MORE
Bristol
Murders

NICOLA SLY

Bristol from the Bath Road, 1829. (Author's collection)

First published 2010

The History Press
The Mill, Brimscombe Port
Stroud, Gloucestershire, GL5 2QG
www.thehistorypress.co.uk

© Nicola Sly, 2010

The right of Nicola Sly to be identified as the Author
of this work has been asserted in accordance with the
Copyrights, Designs and Patents Act 1988.

British Library Cataloguing in Publication Data.
A catalogue record for this book is available from the British Library.

ISBN 978 0 7524 5617 1

Typesetting and origination by The History Press
Printed in Great Britain
Manufacturing managed by Jellyfish Print Solutions Ltd

CONTENTS

ALSO BY THE AUTHOR

A Ghostly Almanac of Devon & Cornwall

Bristol Murders

Cornish Murders (with John Van der Kiste)

Dorset Murders

Hampshire Murders

Herefordshire Murders

More Cornish Murders (with John Van der Kiste)

Murder by Poison: A Casebook of Historic British Murders

Oxfordshire Murders

Shropshire Murders

Somerset Murders (with John Van der Kiste)

West Country Murders (with John Van der Kiste)

Wiltshire Murders

Worcestershire Murders

Bristol from the Cabot Tower. (Author's collection)

INTRODUCTION &
ACKNOWLEDGEMENTS

When writing my book *Bristol Murders*, published by The History Press in 2008, I agonised over which cases to include and which to leave out of the compilation. To me, all seemed equally interesting, but a decision had to be made and several cases had to be excluded. Thus I was delighted to be asked to assemble a second collection of historical true murders from the city of Bristol.

As with the cases in *Bristol Murders*, this selection includes murders that were nationally publicised, as well as those that received only local press coverage in Bristol and the surrounding area. They include the seemingly motiveless murder and suicide involving a brother and sister in Kingswood in 1842, and the 1846 murder of a policeman in St Phillip's, in which the perpetrator had a lucky – albeit temporary – escape from the gallows. There are drunken murders, jealous murders, child murders and those where the killer was never brought to justice, such as the 1899 murder of Ellen Hayball in St Philip's. The penultimate chapter is a brief but tantalising mystery – two seemingly unrelated deaths in different parts of the city in 1915, in which the victims suffered almost identical injuries. Were they simply, in the words of the coroner, '... a most remarkable coincidence'?

As always, there are numerous people to be thanked for their assistance. The staff at the Bristol Reference Library helped enormously with my research, while fellow author Linda Stratmann kindly allowed me to use her picture of Gloucester Penitentiary.

On a personal level, my husband Richard's input was invaluable. He read – and usually corrected – every chapter, as well as acting as chauffeur on my research trips to Bristol and taking some of the photographs. Finally, as always, I must thank my editor at The History Press, Matilda Richards for her help and encouragement.

Every effort has been made to clear copyright, however my apologies to anyone I may have inadvertently missed; I can assure you it was not deliberate but an oversight on my part.

Nicola Sly, 2010

1

'I WILL BEAT YOUR BLOODY BRAINS OUT'

Warmley, 1824

The Tennis Court Tavern in Warmley was very busy on Saturday, 27 November 1824 and, as the night wore on and the drink flowed freely, an argument broke out between some of the customers, one of whom was farm labourer Isaac Gordon. A few days earlier, Gordon's employer, John Brain, had ordered him to impound a loose horse, which was roaming on his land. The horse belonged to another drinker – a man named Francis Britain – who was somewhat aggrieved to find that he would have to pay 2s 6d to retrieve the animal.

Backed by the group of men that he was drinking with, Britain took issue with Isaac Gordon about impounding the horse, saying that he well knew to whom the horse belonged and should have just brought it home. Cross words were exchanged but the matter might have ended there had it not been for the actions of two of Britain's drinking pals, Thomas Wilmot and James Caines, who found a broken clay smoking pipe and began to flick the pieces at Isaac Gordon, apparently with the sole purpose of annoying him.

Eventually, Gordon's patience wore thin and he warned the two lads that, if they didn't stop, he would 'fetch a warrant to them' first thing on Monday morning. 'I will beat your bloody brains out,' James Caines threatened him, at which Gordon decided that it would be safer just to leave the pub and go home.

Thomas Wilmot followed him out and, a few minutes later, Gordon returned to the Tennis Court Tavern, bleeding from a split lip. He now decided that he had better remain in the relative safety of the pub until his tormentors had left.

Minutes after Gordon's return, Francis Britain, his son Isaac, James Caines, Mark Whiting, Robert England and Samuel Peacock decided to call it a night. They ordered six quarts of beer to take away with them and, having begged a candle from the pub landlady to light their way home, they left the pub to walk to Francis Britain's cottage, where they intended to continue drinking. Isaac Gordon waited fifteen minutes or so then set out to walk across the ominously named 'Gibbet Patch' to his lodgings at Mr Brain's farm.

Minutes later, Benjamin Brittain was walking back from Mangotsfield and, as he neared the Tennis Court Tavern, he saw a man lying on the roadside. Brittain called out and, receiving no response from the man, went over to examine him more closely. However, it was extremely dark and Brittain was unable to determine whether the man was dead or just dead drunk. Seconds earlier, Brittain had parted company with his cousin William, who, hearing Benjamin shouting, came to see what the matter was.

Unable to rouse the prone man, Benjamin stayed with him while William Brittain ran to the Tennis Court Tavern, where he hammered on the door until he woke landlord William Blatchley and his son, John. Once a light had been obtained, it was immediately obvious that the man was dead and, as *The Times* was later to relate, '... lying in a gore of blood'. His still-warm body was carried back to a stable at the pub on a borrowed ladder and, when the blood was wiped from the dead man's face, he was immediately recognisable as Isaac Gordon.

Surgeon Mr West was summoned to the pub although he could do nothing but pronounce Gordon dead. A post-mortem examination was later carried out by Samuel Watts, a surgeon from Bitton, who found that, as well as a few small cuts and contusions on Gordon's face, there were two knife wounds on his forehead. However, the cause of his death was a blow to the back of his head, which had produced a skull fracture that was almost six inches long, driving shards of bone deep into his brain. Watts believed that this injury had resulted from a blow from a blunt instrument, such as a pole, stick or staff. In view of the amount of damage to the bone, Watts felt that the blow had been struck with considerable force and that Gordon's death would have been almost instantaneous.

The Tennis Court Tavern, Warmley. (© R. Sly)

For some reason, the police were not informed of the murder until eight o'clock on the morning of 28 November, an omission that doubtless delayed them in catching the culprits. Thus, when coroner Mr W. Joyner Ellis opened the inquest at the Tennis Court Tavern, the jury returned a verdict of 'wilful murder by person or persons unknown'. Yet nobody was in any doubt that one or all of the drinkers at the Tennis Court Tavern were the most likely suspects and the police found plenty of clues to the identity of the murderers when they investigated the scene of the crime.

A 10ft-long pole had been thrust into the hedge, close to where the body had been found. It was quickly traced back to the Tennis Court Tavern where, up until 27 November, it had supported a washing line in the pub's rear garden. A two-bladed penknife lay on the ground nearby, one of its blades broken. There were also numerous footprints, both at the site of the murder and in the back garden of the pub, where the pole had once stood.

On the hedge bank, near to where Isaac Gordon had met his death, was the unmistakeable imprint of human buttocks, as though somebody had sat down on the soft earth. According to Constable John Fusill, the imprint was so clear that it showed that the person whose behind had made it had been wearing corduroy breeches. Not only that, but the breeches had obviously been patched with a corduroy material with much thicker ridges. The constables lifted the entire print and preserved it in wet sawdust, in the hope that a match would be found.

The police rounded up the men who had been present in the pub on 27 November and had been seen by several people arguing with Isaac Gordon. They soon established that Mark Whiting had a pair of corduroy breeches, which had indeed been patched on the seat and exactly matched the imprint in the hedge. The police seized shoes and boots belonging to all of the men and found that those belonging to James Caines and Mark Whiting appeared to have made the footprints near the body, while those of Caines and Isaac Britain matched the prints in the pub garden.

Thomas Wilmot, Francis and Isaac Britain, Robert England, Samuel Peacock, Mark Whiting and James Caines were jointly charged with the wilful murder of Isaac Gordon. However, no evidence could be found against Thomas Wilmot, who was discharged before the case came to court. The remaining six men were tried before Mr Justice Littledale, on 8 April 1825, at the Lent Assizes in Gloucester. They were indicted on three different accounts of 'beating the back of the deceased's head' with what was described in the contemporary newspapers as a 'poll'. The first count stated that James Caines had struck the actual blow in the presence of and with the assistance of the other five defendants. The second count was that all of the defendants struck the deceased and the third was that the blow was struck by person or persons unknown, abetted by the defendants.

The case was prosecuted by Mr Ludlow and Mr Cross, while Mr Phillpotts had been engaged as counsel for the defence for all of the prisoners with the exception of Mark Whiting and James Caines, who were undefended.

The prosecution began by describing the events of 27 November and Mr Ludlow caused almost immediate controversy by claiming that Isaac Gordon had been so afraid of the group of men that he had asked landlord Mr Blatchley if he could have a bed for the night at the pub. According to Mr Ludlow, Blatchley had refused, encouraging Gordon to head off home as soon as possible so that he could lock up for the night. Mr and Mrs Blatchley were later to take the witness stand and both strongly denied this.

The court heard from several of the pub's customers, who – as might be expected in a crowded and noisy room – had all seen and heard slightly different things. Francis Rogers had first seen the group of men, including Isaac Gordon, drinking together quite peaceably, passing around a shared mug. Rogers had heard the subsequent argument but swore that James Caines was the only person to 'give an ill word'.

William Hiscocks had witnessed the pipe throwing and insisted that it was started by Thomas Wilmot, although James Caines alone had threatened violence towards Gordon when he told him to stop. However, Joseph Pratton had heard Robert England threatening Isaac Gordon and also stated that, when Thomas Wilmot followed Gordon out of the pub, England accompanied him. Pratton's version of events was corroborated by Joseph Henley.

Landlady Mrs Blatchley had seen only James Caines flicking pieces of pipe at Isaac Gordon and had threatened to 'stop the tap' if he didn't desist. According to Mrs Blatchley, the Britains left the pub first with Caines and Whiting, while Robert England and Samuel Peacock stayed a few minutes longer, waiting for the beer they had ordered. Mrs Blatchley's son, John, agreed with what she said, although he believed that Joseph Pratton left with the Britains, Caines and Whiting. Most of the witnesses agreed that, of the six defendants, only Isaac Britain was 'a little elevated by liquor'.

The prosecution next called Hannah Lewis, who lived with her husband in the cottage outside which Gordon's body had been found. Although Edward Lewis was asleep at the time of the murder and so heard nothing, Hannah was sitting sewing and related hearing the voices of three or four men. Mrs Lewis heard a faint cry of 'Murder!' followed by the sounds of something or somebody being beaten, which she described in court as sounding like somebody beating an ass. She heard no other cries or screams and, when the beating sounds stopped, she told the court that she had heard men laughing, as well as someone calling out what appeared to be a name. She admitted that she had not heard the name clearly and that, although she was sufficiently perturbed by what she heard to get up and lock her door, she had not investigated the noises further and had known nothing about the murder until she and her husband were later roused by Benjamin Brittain.

Elizabeth Ponting, who lived next door, was able to be a little more specific. She too heard the faint cry of 'Murder!' and the sound of men's voices, followed by laughter. Someone had clearly said, 'There thee be'est ...' and she had distinctly heard the name 'Bob' mentioned.

The prosecution also called Jonathon Ford, who told the court that on 27 November he had seen Robert England using a knife to trim his fingernails. 'That's a pretty knife, Bob,' Ford remarked and England immediately offered to sell it to him. Ford stated that he had inspected the knife closely before deciding that he didn't want to buy it. Although he could not be absolutely certain, Ford believed that the knife found near where Gordon was attacked was very similar to England's knife, apart from the fact that England's knife had not had a broken blade when he saw it.

The next witnesses to testify were those who had seen the footprints at the murder site and in the pub garden. Thomas Waters and Constables George Haskins and John Fusill admitted that there had been heavy rain and some snow around the time of the murder and, as a consequence of the weather and the hordes of curious people who flocked to view the murder site, many of the footprints had been obliterated before they could be physically compared with the defendants' shoes. However, all three witnesses swore that, on first viewing the prints, they had particularly noticed a T-shaped pattern of nails, which corresponded exactly to the sole of James Caines's boots. Additionally, all three men stated that the impression in the soft earth was identical to the patched breeches worn by Mark Whiting on his arrest, which were produced in court for comparison to the preserved patch of soil.

Haskins also told the court that Caines, Whiting and Peacock all had spots of what looked like blood on their clothes when they were arrested. Caines insisted that the stains on his coat were pitch from the boiler, while Whiting said that the blood had come from a briar scratch on his nose. Samuel Fusill, the son of the constable, testified that he had seen Whiting scratch his nose and that it had bled quite heavily but Fusill insisted that there had already been two spots of blood on Whiting's coat before he was scratched. Peacock attributed the bloodstains on his clothes to a fight some months before the murder.

Surgeon Samuel Watts described Gordon's injuries to the court, agreeing that the pole could have caused his fatal head wound and that the knife with the broken blade could have made the stab wounds in his forehead, the blade breaking when it made contact with the bone. The pole was produced in court with the defence pointing out that it was a very large and heavy weapon and asking the doctor if it was even possible for one man alone to have managed to hit somebody with it. Watts stated that it was, adding that it would be easier if the attacker was standing in an elevated position, such as on top of a hedge bank. The constables had already stated that they had found footprints on top of the hedge bank at the side of the lane where Gordon's body was found, along with some damage to the hedge itself. There had been a large pool of blood indicating exactly where Gordon had been standing when he was hit and the distance between the blood and the hedge bank corresponded with the length of the pole.

Having heard the medical evidence, the prosecution rested. Although all of the accused except Caines and Whiting were defended, their defence counsel seems to have done very little apart from calling a single character witness for Samuel Peacock. Caines and Whiting had both made statements, each accusing the other of committing the murder and their statements were admitted as evidence. Whiting said that he had known Gordon for twelve years and never had so much as a cross word with him. Caines, on the other hand, swore that Whiting had confessed to him that he alone had murdered Gordon, saying that he had actually intended to murder Francis Rogers.

It was left for Mr Justice Littledale to summarise the evidence for the jury. Speaking for more than three hours, Littledale first addressed the motive for Gordon's murder, saying that nothing had been stolen from the victim and – aside from the argument in the pub – none of the defendants seemed to have born any previous ill-feeling towards him.

The quarrel in the pub seemed to have mainly involved James Caines and, according to the judge, it was quite beyond belief that, even if Caines had born any animosity towards Gordon as a result of their argument, he could have persuaded his co-defendants to assist him in carrying out the murder. Littledale told the jury that the fact that the defendants were together in the pub was irrelevant, as was their meeting at Francis Britain's cottage later that night. The first meeting had been coincidental, whereas the second was a regular occurrence and simply represented a desire to carry on drinking after hours.

The testimony of Mrs Lewis and Mrs Ponting, who had heard voices near the scene of the murder, was also to be treated with caution, since neither woman could be sure exactly how many voices she had heard. As for the laughter, Littledale said that he could scarcely believe that men would laugh out loud after having brutally killed somebody.

The judge then looked at the evidence against each of the men individually. Against Robert England was the possible ownership of the knife used to stab Isaac Gordon and the fact that Mrs Ponting professed to have clearly heard someone calling the name 'Bob'. However, even if the knife had belonged to England, that didn't necessarily implicate him in the murder, particularly as the stab wounds were not the cause of death. In addition, Robert England was carrying the jug of beer when he left the pub and had later arrived at Francis Britain's house with the jug, from which not a drop of beer had been spilled.

The evidence was strongest against James Caines and Mark Whiting, stated the judge. Caines had threatened Isaac Gordon, blood had been found on his clothes and his boots had matched the footprints at the murder scene and in the pub garden. Likewise Mark Whiting, whose footprints were also found at the murder scene, along with an imprint of his breeches.

Isaac Britain's footprints were found in the pub garden but there was no proof that he had been at the murder scene and, even if he had assisted in uprooting the post knowing what it was to be used for, that would only make him an accessory before the fact and not a principal in the murder. As for Samuel Peacock and Francis Britain, the only evidence against them was that they were part of the group of drinkers at the pub. Littledale therefore suggested to the jury that they should be acquitted.

The jury deliberated for ten minutes before returning their verdict. Francis and Isaac Britain, Samuel Peacock and Robert England were found 'not guilty', while Mark Whiting and James Caines were found 'guilty' of the wilful murder of Isaac Gordon.

Mr Justice Littledale turned to Caines and Whiting and asked them if there was any reason why sentence of death should not be passed.

'Nothing at all,' said Whiting, while Caines replied, 'Only that I am innocent.'

The two men were removed from court looking pale and haggard and, as they left, Whiting muttered something, heard only by those sitting nearest to the dock. Those who did hear what he said were later to swear that he had taken sole responsibility for killing Isaac Gordon, saying that all of his co-defendants were innocent. However, since the trial took place on 8 April and Whiting and Caines were executed at Gloucester Prison on 11 April, there was little time to ponder his apparent confession.

Note: Given the age of this case, there are perhaps not surprisingly some discrepancies between the various sources. In some contemporary accounts of the murder, Francis and Isaac Britain are alternatively named Britton while the pub landlord is named as both Blatchley and Blaxley. There is also some confusion about Benjamin and William Brittain. Their name is spelled both Brittain and Britain in the contemporary newspapers and, if the latter is correct, it is possible that they were related to the two defendants Francis and Isaac Britain. I have been unable to confirm any relationship between the four men. Finally, it is not absolutely clear whether surgeons Mr West and Mr Watts are in fact the same person, the former name being a typographical error in the newspapers.

2

'THE DEVIL LEAVES HIS FRIENDS IN THE LURCH'

Stapleton, 1836

Eighteen-year-old Sarah Lewis was in service as a lady's maid to a family in Bath when she met and quickly fell in love with Samuel Charles Bartlett. Bartlett was a seemingly respectable cabinet maker and, when he proposed marriage shortly after their first meeting, Sarah was only too eager to accept. She left her job in Bath and returned to her home in Monmouth, where she informed her parents about her impending nuptials and, with the help of her mother, Mary, began organising her wedding.

Neither Mary Lewis nor her husband, James, were too keen on their prospective son-in-law but Sarah was determined and, realising the futility of any argument, her parents reluctantly accepted that their daughter had her heart set on marrying him and made the couple a generous wedding gift of £47, suggesting to Bartlett that the money could be used to furnish a little house for the newlyweds. It was mentioned at the time that, on her mother's death, Sarah would receive a further £50.

Having married in Monmouth on 16 August 1836, the Bartletts spent a couple of days there before taking a coach to Bristol where they were to live. The ink was barely dry on their marriage certificate when James and Mary Lewis received a letter from their daughter and son-in-law concerning a burglary that Bartlett had been accused of committing while in Monmouth.

It is not recorded exactly when James and Mary found out that, far from being a respectable cabinet maker, their new son-in-law had actually given up his trade a year earlier to become a fairground performer, a man variously described in the contemporary newspapers as an actor, a comedian and a showman. Having a son who suffered from a problem with his eyesight and, guessing that Bartlett would be working at Bristol Fair, Mary decided to visit her daughter in Bristol to try and sort out her problems and, at the same time, take her son for treatment at the hospital on Guinea Street. She and the boy left Monmouth on 5 September, intending to stay with friends in Bristol as they had done many times in the past.

In the early afternoon of Saturday 10 September, several people heard the sound of a pistol or gun shot coming from an area near the Mason's Arms public house in Stapleton. However, the last day of Bristol Fair was in full swing and, knowing that the performers often fired pistols into the air to attract crowds to their shows, nobody gave the noise a second thought until, at just before half-past two, Emma Davis decided to walk into Stapleton.

Her quickest route was through the back garden of her cottage then down a steep bank into Lippet's Lane, a narrow footpath bordered on both sides by overgrown banks of stinging nettles. She had walked only a few yards when she came across the partially clothed body of a woman lying on her back diagonally across the lane. Emma was too frightened to approach the body but ran back home, shouting to her husband, Robert, that there was a woman lying dead or drunk on the lane. Along with a neighbour, Mr Bridgman, Robert went to investigate, finding the body of a middle-aged woman who had apparently been shot in the back of her head.

Leaving Mr Bridgman with the body, Robert alerted several of his neighbours and soon a small crowd of people had gathered, among them Robert Bedford, the landlord of the nearby public house, the Mason's Arms. Although Bedford didn't know the woman's identity, he realised that she had been drinking gin and water in his pub only a short while earlier, when she was accompanied by a young man. Bedford suggested that the woman was conveyed to the pub and several of the crowd helped to carry her still-warm body there. At Bedford's suggestion, Robert Davis scrambled to the top of the 7ft-high wall bordering one side of the lane, from where he spotted a woman's gingham umbrella lying in the field adjoining the path. With a little help from the crowd, Davis was boosted over the wall to retrieve the umbrella, which was taken to the pub along with the woman's straw bonnet, found lying on the ground near her body.

The Mason's Arms, Stapleton. (© R. Sly)

Dr Alloway was summoned to the pub where he examined the unidentified body, finding a gunshot wound on the back of her head. The wound was at the very base of the woman's skull and, on examining her bonnet, Alloway noted that it was blackened with gunpowder, from which he concluded that the shot that killed her had been fired at point-blank range. The woman's pockets still held a small purse containing 4s 6d in coins, along with a receipt for the purchase of a shawl and, although her gloves had been rolled down, she was still wearing rings on her fingers.

The news of the presence of the unidentified body at the Mason's Arms spread around the area like wildfire and people flocked to the pub to inspect and try to identify the corpse. Among them was Samuel Bartlett, who arrived on the day after the body was found. Robert Bedford and his wife Harriet immediately recognised him as the young man who had accompanied the deceased to the pub on the day of her murder. The landlord had covered the body with a sheet and, as Bartlett approached the bed on which the woman now rested, Bedford stepped forward to turn down the sheet and expose her face. He had barely begun to lift the sheet when Bartlett exclaimed, 'My God! It is my wife's mother.'

With Bartlett slumped in a chair apparently on the verge of fainting, Robert Bedford began questioning him about the woman. Bartlett told him that her name was Mrs Lewis, although he said that he didn't know her first name. Having identified a ring that the dead woman wore on her finger, Bartlett seemed suddenly keen to leave, telling Bedford that he had to go and meet his wife.

PC John Nichols was downstairs in the pub and Bedford sent his wife to fetch him. Nichols would not allow Bartlett to leave, even though Bartlett pleaded to be allowed to go to his wife, who he said was on her way to the pub at that very moment. He eventually agreed somewhat reluctantly to stay put, telling Nichols, 'I shall not run away.' He asked if he might have some brandy and Nichols escorted him downstairs and obtained some for him.

When Sarah Bartlett arrived at the pub, she was taken upstairs to view the body, immediately falling into a faint when she recognised it as that of her mother. Taken downstairs to her husband when she had recovered her senses, Sarah looked at him and asked sorrowfully, 'Oh, Bartlett, how could you do it?'

Bartlett stared back at her incredulously. 'What? You accuse me of the murder too?'

'I do, Bartlett,' Sarah replied. 'You are the man that shot my mother.'

With Bartlett still detained at the Mason's Arms, a warrant was hurriedly obtained from magistrate Revd Mirehouse to search his lodgings in Barton Street and, when it was presented to him, Bartlett handed over his keys without protest. At his house, Sergeant Thomas Waltham and PC John Alexander found three boxes, one of which was locked. Having procured the services of a locksmith to open the third box, the policemen found two pistols – a horse pistol and a smaller double-barrelled pistol, which had obviously been recently fired. There were several items of clothing in the box, including a brown coat, a shirt and a pair of blue striped trousers, all of which had grains of gunpowder in their pockets. Also found in the coat pocket was a short, blackened stick that fitted perfectly into the barrels of the smaller pistol.

An inquest was opened at the Mason's Arms by coroner William Joyner Ellis on the Monday after the murder, at which Samuel Bartlett was in attendance. Described as '... rather a good looking, light complexioned young man with something of a rakish appearance which attaches to persons of his profession', Bartlett seemed almost to try and control the proceedings.

He first asked the coroner if he might be permitted a pencil and a piece of paper, which the coroner allowed, directing that his handcuffs should be removed to allow him to make notes. At that point, the inquest had already heard from a witness named Mary Tickell, who knew Bartlett from his performances in the shows and, having seen the dead body, recognised it to be his mother-in-law. Now that he had his pencil and paper, Bartlett asked the coroner if Mrs Tickell's testimony might be repeated, claiming that it differed from a statement that she had given to the magistrates on the previous day.

'I know nothing of what passed yesterday and, if you will be advised by me, you will not press your request,' the coroner warned Bartlett, adding, 'At present, nothing is proved but the identity of the body.'

Robert Davis was next to speak, followed by landlady Harriet Bedford, who told the inquest that Bartlett and Mrs Lewis had been drinking in the Mason's Arms together shortly before her body was found. Harriet related that Bartlett had bought two small glasses of gin and water and that he did not seem very cheerful, refusing to respond to Harriet's attempts at polite conversation.

Harriet described the clothes that Bartlett was wearing at the time and was able to positively identify him, having particularly noticed that he was missing a finger from one hand. She told the inquest that, while in the pub, Bartlett had asked to borrow a knife to 'cut a bit of stick' and, having been provided with a knife, spent some time alone in the pub yard before returning it. Once again, Bartlett suggested that the coroner questioned Mrs Bedford further to try and find out what she felt was peculiar about him, saying that not being cheerful might arise from being concerned about business or some other matter.

The coroner insisted that they must confine themselves to facts, at which Bartlett nodded politely to Mrs Bedford, saying, 'I trust the landlady may always meet with smiling customers.'

One of the next people to testify was sixteen-year-old Henry Lovell, who worked for Mr Ingleton, the travelling theatre owner who also employed Samuel Bartlett. Lovell told the inquest that the performers would frequently fire pistols into the air to attract people to their shows. He had often purchased gunpowder for Bartlett but, on the day before the murder, Bartlett had given him a penny and asked him to buy some bullets for his pistol.

Lovell asked if he should take the pistol with him to ensure that he bought the right ammunition but instead Bartlett took a small piece of bread and butter from another theatre employee and rolled it into a ball, which he fitted into his pistol and then gave to Lovell as an indication of the correct size. He asked Lovell not to mention the purchase of bullets to his wife, telling him that, if Sarah asked, he was to say that he was buying caps. Lovell tried to purchase the requested bullets but was unable to find any. 'It is of no consequence,' Bartlett told him.

When Lovell had finished his testimony, Bartlett again began to argue, telling the coroner that he was the leading man in the show and it was his job to make as much noise as possible to draw in the crowds. Since pistols made more noise if they had something in them other than gunpowder, he had asked the boy to obtain some bullets. The reason that he had asked Lovell not to tell his wife, said Bartlett, was that they had 'had a few words'.

Once again, the coroner advised Bartlett not to go into statements of that kind.

Dr Alloway had conducted a post-mortem examination on the woman, at which he extracted eight flattened pieces of shot from the area between her scalp and her skull and a further four pieces of shot from her brain. The fact that there was only one entrance wound confirmed Alloway's first impression that the woman had been shot at very close range, the shots penetrating several major blood vessels which, according to the doctor, would have resulted in instant death. Once Alloway had given his evidence, Bartlett asked the coroner to call several witnesses, who he insisted would be able to vouch for his movements on the day of the murder.

Mr Joyner Ellis advised him against such a course of action, although he told Bartlett that he was willing to call the witnesses if Bartlett insisted. Bartlett did, stating that, if these witnesses were called now, they could be bound over to appear again in future but if they were not called then he ran the risk of not being able to locate them again.

Bartlett named three witnesses he specifically wished to be called but only one of the three – the Bartletts' landlady, Mrs Ann Stock – could be found. Before Mrs Stock could address the inquest, magistrate Revd Mirehouse asked Bartlett if he would like his own statement to be read out. Bartlett decided that he would but the coroner immediately advised him against it and, this time, Bartlett was willing to accept his advice.

In the event, Mrs Stock's testimony was rather less helpful to Bartlett than he had obviously anticipated, since she told the inquest that he had left her house at between midday and one o'clock and not returned until ten o'clock in the evening.

The coroner's jury deliberated in private for around thirty minutes before advising the coroner that they had agreed on a verdict of 'wilful murder against Samuel Bartlett.' The news was broken to Bartlett, with the coroner advising him to make every effort to appoint a defence counsel before his trial. He was then removed to Lawford's Gate Gaol, prior to being transferred by coach to Gloucester Prison.

Bartlett was later to write to his wife:

Dear wife, I entreat of you to set aside the past and confine yourself to my present awful situation. You are well aware I have no friend near to assist me. I therefore call on you as in duty bound to render me all the assistance in your power. If you can possibly remain here until next week to see my mother, do so. Were I guilty of the dreadful crime I am charged with I know not what my sufferings would be. Even now, at times, my brain seems bewildered. I much wish to see your poor distracted father and hope that he will not leave without. I call upon you by all the tender feelings of a wife, if you have any – by every tie, sacred, human and divine – not to desert your husband in this trying hour.

However, time is precious; I therefore conclude begging to be kindly remembered, with every sentiment of affection, to your unhappy father and believe me ever your affectionate, truly innocent and falsely accused, unhappy husband.

Bartlett was brought to trial at Gloucester Assizes on 6 April 1837, before Mr Baron Bolland. The case was prosecuted by Mr Greaves and Mr Talbot, while Bartlett was defended by Mr Alexander.

As he had at the inquest, Bartlett seemed confident to the point of being cocksure. Asked how he pleaded, he told the court, 'With the word of God on my heart and lips, I can truly say I am not guilty.' Throughout his trial, Bartlett jotted down notes and consulted with his counsel, suggesting questions for him to ask. Occasionally, he nonchalantly sucked on an orange or took sips from a glass of beer.

The prosecution called numerous witnesses, which included James Lewis and Jane Pattison, the woman with whom Mary Lewis usually stayed whenever she visited Bristol. Mrs Pattison told the court that Mary Lewis had been determined to attend Bristol Fair to see for herself if what she had been told about her son-in-law's job was true. Both Mrs Pattison and Bartlett's landlady, Mrs Stock, told the court that, during Mrs Lewis's stay at Bristol, she had dined with her daughter and son-in-law several times and that the three appeared to get on well together.

Henry Lovell testified on being asked to buy bullets for Bartlett's pistol and Emma and Robert Davis related finding Mrs Lewis's body in Lippet's Lane. (Robert fainted while giving his evidence and was eventually helped from the witness box to return and complete his testimony the following day.)

The old Gloucester Penitentiary (from an eighteenth-century print). (By kind permission of Linda Stratmann)

The prosecution then called several witnesses who had either seen Bartlett drinking in the Mason's Arms with his mother-in-law on the day of her death or had seen them walking into Lippet's Lane together after leaving the pub. Through his counsel, Bartlett challenged the evidence of several of these witnesses. Mr Alexander questioned one pub customer at length about her eyesight, suggesting that she was unable to see properly without glasses. When Harriet Bedford took the stand, Mr Alexander disputed her testimony, saying that it differed from statements that she had previously given to the magistrates. 'Have a care, Mrs Bedford,' he urged. 'Remember that this man's life is at stake.'

By the time the court had heard Dr Alloway's medical evidence it was past nine o'clock at night and the judge adjourned the proceedings until the following morning. The now recovered Robert Davis was the first witness, followed by landlord Robert Bedford, who informed the court that, as a result of a description of Mrs Lewis's drinking companion given to the police by himself and his wife, a policeman had been despatched to Stroud to question a possible suspect. Inspector Joseph Jerrard of the Bristol Police reassured the court that the suspect at Stroud had turned out to bear only a passing resemblance to the man seen with Mrs Lewis and, when Bartlett arrived at the pub the next day, he was immediately recognised as having visited the pub with the victim immediately before her death.

Labourer John Needham testified to finding a percussion cap and gun shot in the outside toilet of the pub on the morning after the murder. Dr Alloway was recalled to state that he had compared the shot with that recovered from the victim's brain and that it appeared almost identical.

The court next heard from the policemen involved in the investigation, followed by Revd Mirehouse, who had taken Bartlett's statement in the pub after the body had been identified. Mr Alexander questioned whether Bartlett had been properly cautioned and also pointed out that there had been several other people in the room at the time, many of whom had already made statements in Bartlett's hearing. In spite of Mr Alexander's protests, the judge ruled that Bartlett had signed his statement and it was therefore admissible.

In his statement, Bartlett went into great detail about everyone he had met and spoken to on the day of the murder and the clothes he had been wearing. He made very little mention of Mary Lewis, apart from saying that he had been out on the morning of the murder and that she was at his lodgings visiting his wife when he arrived home. 'I went no way with the deceased,' Bartlett insisted, stating that his mother-in-law had left his home alone at about twenty-past one and that he had stayed at home with his wife until half-past two.

Once Bartlett's statement had been admitted as evidence, the prosecution rested. Bartlett and Alexander began a discussion about whether or not to call any witnesses for his defence, finally deciding that they would not do so. Mr Alexander was on the verge of commencing his defence when prosecution counsel Mr Greaves asked for permission to introduce another witness, who had just arrived from Bristol.

'What is he to prove?' asked the judge.

'I understand, my lord, that he will prove that, on the day of the murder, a person answering the description of the prisoner applied at his shop to purchase some shot of the same kind as that used in the pistol.'

'I cannot refuse to hear him,' decreed the judge, at which Nathaniel Puddy was ushered into court. However, far from proving anything, Puddy took one look at the defendant and stated that Bartlett was not the man who had visited his shop.

Finally, it was Mr Alexander's turn to address the court. Bartlett was charged with a very heinous crime, admitted Alexander – the murder of a woman who he was bound by every tie of relationship, as well as by humanity, to cherish and protect. That Mrs Lewis had been murdered was indisputable, said Alexander, yet there was nothing to suggest that her death had been at the hands of his client.

What possible motive could Bartlett have had for killing his mother-in-law, asked Alexander? Barely a month before, he had received the princely sum of £47 on his marriage, in addition to which he had been earning good wages from his work. There was no financial motive for the murder, neither was there any question of anger or revenge, since numerous witnesses had testified that Bartlett and Mrs Lewis appeared to be on good terms.

Alexander pointed out that among the eyewitnesses who claimed to have seen Samuel Bartlett with Mary Lewis immediately prior to Mrs Lewis's murder, there had been considerable discrepancy in describing both Bartlett and the clothes he was wearing at the time. There had even been argument about whether or not he was missing a finger and, between those who believed that he was, exactly which finger was missing. Mr Alexander urged the jury not to rely on the evidence of identification, asking them to give his client the benefit of any doubts they might have. 'Say but the word "Guilty" and the consequences of your judgement are irretrievable,' he told them, reminding them that Samuel Bartlett had co-operated fully with the police in giving them his house keys and telling them where his pistols were located and that he had presented himself voluntarily at the pub out of concern for the whereabouts of his mother-in-law.

Could Mrs Lewis's killer possibly have been that cool and calm? There is a well-known saying, continued Alexander; 'The devil leaves his friends in the lurch.' If Bartlett was indeed guilty of the crime with which he was accused then his emotions would surely have betrayed that guilt.

'It is better that ten guilty men should escape than one innocent man be unjustly sacrificed,' concluded Mr Alexander, his voice cracking with emotion and tears welling in his eyes as he told the jury; 'Gentlemen, I leave his life in your hands.'

In a three-hour-long summary of the case, Mr Baron Bolland reiterated Mr Alexander's comments about evidence of identity, describing a trial that he had recently presided over in which a female defendant had been positively identified by no less than eleven separate witnesses but had eventually been acquitted when the evidence had conclusively proved the guilt of another woman. The judge also cautioned the jury to give the defendant the benefit of any doubts they might entertain.

When the jury retired to commence their deliberations, Bartlett chatted calmly with his defence counsel and the governor of Gloucester Prison, telling them that he felt a tremendous strength, which he attributed to knowing that he was inno- cent and having a clear conscience. He was therefore most surprised when the jury returned to court after twenty-eight minutes to pronounce him 'Guilty'.

Asked if he had anything to say before sentence was passed, Bartlett launched into a long, theatrical speech reasserting his innocence, saying, 'You, my jury, have erred but I daresay you have given your verdict conscientiously and I forgive you freely from my soul.' Bartlett continued to say that he realised the futility of pro- testing his innocence but stated that he would soon be facing a far more discerning judge and that he went to his Father's mansion in Heaven with a clear conscience. He instructed Mr Baron Bolland, 'Proceed, my lord, to pronounce your sentence – your sentence unjust and unmerited – and you will see how, with the consciousness of innocence, I will brave my death. You shall see that I will never cease to call down from righteous Heaven imprecations on the head of her murderer.'

The judge went on to pronounce sentence of death on Samuel Bartlett, telling him that, throughout the entire trial, there had only been one brief moment when he personally had doubted Bartlett's guilt. A witness named Thomas Cook, who knew Bartlett well, had testified to seeing him at twenty minutes to three on the afternoon of the murder, at a distance of almost three and a half miles from where the body of Mrs Lewis was found. If this sighting was accurate then Bartlett couldn't possibly have committed the murder, but the jury had obviously discounted Cook's testimony on the assumption that he was mistaken about the time. Saying that he was completely satis- fied that the jury had reached the correct verdict, Mr Baron Bolland sentenced Bartlett to death, ending with the traditional words '... the Lord have mercy on your soul.'

'The just God most assuredly will,' rejoined Bartlett, pausing only to shake hands with his attorney and a friend before marching resolutely out of the court, his head held high. Tragically, in another part of the city, at the very moment that Samuel Bartlett was receiving his sentence, his wife Sarah was being delivered of a dead pre- mature baby by Dr Alloway.

Almost immediately, Bartlett's defence counsel applied for a stay of execution on the grounds that they had new evidence that would prove an alibi for Bartlett for the time of the murder. Three sworn affidavits were submitted to Mr Baron Bolland for his consideration and Bolland promised that, although his own opinions of the case hadn't changed, he would forward the documentation to the Secretary of State for his urgent attention.

The condemned man was not told of the efforts being made to save his life until an official letter was received to say that they had been unsuccessful and that there was no hope of a pardon. In the run up to his execution, Bartlett maintained his extraor- dinary composure. He was visited by his wife, his father-in-law and his brother, insisting to them that he was innocent of the murder of Mary Lewis and, in spite of attempts from several clergymen to persuade him to confess his sins he went to the gallows vehemently denying his guilt.

He gave a long and impassioned speech to that effect from the scaffold, ending with his last words, 'I am an injured man'. Then, watched by a crowd of more than 5,000 people, he dropped the handkerchief that he held in his hand as a signal to the executioner to proceed. His last requests were that his head be sent to a phrenologist and his body to the local infirmary, where it might be used for the good of society.

Although twenty-three-year-old Samuel Charles Bartlett protested his innocence literally to his last breath, after his death the newspapers printed a statement made by Jane Pattison, the woman with whom Mary Lewis had stayed on her visit to Bristol. Mrs Pattison's statement had not been presented in court since it amounted to hearsay, detailing a conversation between Mary Lewis and Mrs Pattison that allegedly took place two days before the murder.

Mrs Pattison insisted that Mary Lewis had arrived home on the Thursday before her death 'all over in a tremble from head to foot.' When Mrs Pattison asked what had upset her so, Mary told her, 'Bartlett has been making a proposal to me that I don't half like.' She told Mrs Pattison that her son-in-law had suggested that they went for a walk alone together on Saturday.

Mrs Pattison advised Mary to ask Bartlett where he was intending to go and why. This Mary Lewis did the next day, reporting back to Mrs Pattison that her son-in-law wished her to accompany him to Winterbourne, where he told her that he could obtain some money. Jane offered to go with her but Mary said that Bartlett would be angry if he knew that she had told anyone about the walk. She believed that Bartlett had incurred a debt of some sort and that he wanted her to sign for it. Against the wishes of Mrs Pattison and her daughter, Mary Lewis went to meet her son-in-law on the day of her death, taking her reading glasses with her and assuring her hostess that she was not about to be duped into signing for anything.

The newspapers also printed an allegation that, when visited by his wife in Lawford's Gate Prison, Bartlett had asked her to purchase some oxalic acid and smuggle it into the prison should he be sentenced to death. He suggested to Sarah that they should both take the poison and die together. Yet, when James Lewis visited his son-in-law and informed him that he forgave him, Samuel Bartlett told him that he did not want or need his forgiveness, since he had done nothing to injure him. Lewis asked Bartlett if he knew who had murdered his wife and Bartlett replied enigmatically that, should Lewis live a few more years, it would come to light. 'You will then know that I died a martyr for another man's crime,' Bartlett told his father-in-law.

It was intimated at the time that Bartlett may have had an accomplice in the murder of Mary Lewis and that he might have arranged for her to be killed, rather than firing the actual shot that ended her life. This theory was given some credence by the fact that, at the time of her death, Mary Lewis should have had between five and seven sovereigns in her purse rather than the mere 4s 6d that it was found to contain. A man Bartlett referred to only as 'Mr Brown' was known to have been at Bartlett's lodgings on the morning of the murder and to have left there soon after Mary Lewis. Bartlett himself was known to have a purse containing five sovereigns on the morning of the murder yet, on his arrest the next day, was carrying only three. Had he paid 'Mr Brown' to kill his mother-in-law, relying on Sarah receiving money on her death as a beneficiary from her will?

While Bartlett was in the condemned cell, an anonymous letter with a London postmark was received by the governor of Gloucester Prison proclaiming Bartlett's innocence and stating that the writer's husband, since deceased, had murdered Mrs Lewis. The writer of the letter was never traced, neither was the identity of 'Mr Brown' ever confirmed.

Note: Bartlett's given name appears to be Samuel Charles Bartlett, although some newspapers of the time record it as Charles Samuel Bartlett and he appears to have used both forenames. (He was married under the name of Charles Bartlett but later signed a letter to his wife as Samuel.) The contemporary newspapers use both names equally but early accounts of the murder give Bartlett's name as Robert Bartlett.

3

'I CANNOT HELP BUT TROUBLE'

Kingswood, Bitton, 1842

At half-past six on the morning of 31 March 1842, Hester and Isaac Peacock of Kingswood in the parish of Bitton were disturbed by a shout of 'Murder!' from the cottage occupied by Samuel Cook and his sister Edith. Isaac went to investigate and found fifty-year-old Samuel Cook lying on the cottage floor in a pool of blood, his throat cut from ear to ear.

The Cooks were rumoured to keep money at home and Peacock jumped to the conclusion that somebody had broken in with the intention of robbing them and attacked Samuel. The door leading onto the stairs was open and there was no sign of Edith Cook and, fearing that the intruders might still be in the cottage, Peacock ran for help.

Almost immediately he met Abraham Fry, who had been delivering milk in the area when he also heard the desperate cry from the Cooks' cottage and was on his way to see what the matter was. Together, Cook and Fry went back to the cottage and, as they did, they spotted Edith Cook lying among the cabbage stumps in the garden, about ten yards from the door, her throat also cut.

Edith Cook was beyond all help but when the two men went back into the cottage to check on Samuel, they found that he was still alive, even though his throat was cut so deeply that his vertebrae were exposed. Samuel seemed determined to speak but could only make a ghastly gurgling sound. A doctor was summoned and, while awaiting his arrival, the two men gave what comfort they could to the severely injured man. It was only when they tried to raise him to a sitting position that they discovered a bloody razor still clutched tightly in his hand.

Surgeon Richard James Biggs arrived at the cottage at about 7.15 a.m. and stitched up the terrible wound in Samuel Cook's throat. Although weak through loss of blood, once the wound was closed, Samuel was able to speak and told the three men, 'I did it – I cut her throat and then my own.' Although every effort was made to save Samuel's life, he died within a couple of hours of being found.

Bitton, 1916. (Author's collection)

The cottage near the church where the brother and sister lived had been in their family for more than a hundred years and had been occupied by Edith and Samuel for about ten years, ever since the death of Samuel's wife from typhus fever. Edith and Samuel had both caught the fever that ultimately killed Samuel's wife and, although they survived, Edith had been quite out of her mind for some time after falling ill, while Samuel was left with nervous depression so severe that he was forced to give up his job as a timber hewer. However, Samuel owned a few properties in the area, the rent from which was sufficient to support him and his sister and they supplemented their income when necessary by selling potatoes from their garden.

Indeed, a considerable amount of money was found when the house was searched after the deaths. A box in Edith Cook's room contained eight sovereigns and more than £41 in silver coins, which had been neatly packed into £1 bundles. Another box yielded £2 19s in silver and nearly 4s in copper and there was a shilling and a few coppers in Samuel's trouser pockets.

An inquest into the deaths was opened at the King's Arms by coroner Mr W. Joyner Ellis. The proceedings dealt with the finding and identification of the two bodies, hearing from Abraham Fry and Isaac Peacock. When the razor belonging to Samuel Cook was produced for the inspection of the inquest jury, Peacock was reprimanded by the coroner for levity and improper conduct after he asked the jury, 'Which of you be going to shave with the razor?'

The inquest then heard from surgeon Mr Biggs who, as well as dealing with the aftermath of the tragedy, had also been the Cooks' regular doctor. Biggs told the inquest that he had never observed any signs of insanity whatsoever in Samuel Cook, although he added that Edith had been insane in the past after her bout of typhus fever. The surgeon stated that Edith Cook's throat had apparently been cut either while she sitting or standing close to the cottage fireplace. She had a single wound that was between three and four inches long, which had severed her carotid artery and jugular vein. Biggs believed that she had been dead for between sixty and ninety minutes when he arrived at the cottage. He gave his opinion that, although her death would have been almost instantaneous, she could probably have staggered out of the cottage and into the garden before dying from loss of blood. Although Biggs had not noticed it on his initial examination of Edith's body, when he came to conduct the post-mortem examination, he found that a night cap had been stuffed into the open wound in her throat, which would have temporarily slowed the loss of blood. Fear, said Mr Biggs, could have a powerful effect on the body and he recalled a particular case from his earlier career in which the wing of a hospital in London caught fire. One particular patient, who had been bedridden and unable to move for several years, was so terrified that he got up and ran away.

Samuel Cook had less serious injuries than those of his sister since, although his cut was deep, he had somehow managed to avoid all of the major blood vessels in his throat. A reporter from the *Bristol Mercury* theorised that after Edith managed to escape the house, Samuel followed her into the garden and, hearing her desperate cries of 'Murder!', realised that his deed was bound to be discovered and went back to the house to cut his own throat.

The jury debated for almost an hour but were unable to reach a verdict, so the inquest was adjourned and, when it resumed on 5 April, the coroner heard from several witnesses about the relationship between Samuel Cook and his sister. Both of the Cooks were very religious and regularly attended the local Methodist chapel. At the first sitting of the inquest, it was stated that Samuel and Edith had always 'lived comfortably' together but now the coroner heard from a stream of witnesses who were prepared to state that this wasn't necessarily true. It was generally agreed that Edith could be very hot tempered and prone to sulking.

Samuel was known as a kind and steady man, but had recently complained to several people that he felt 'poorly'. Whereas most of the witnesses agreed that Samuel was suffering from little more than a cold, it was stated that Edith had suffered from severe pain in her hips and legs. Samuel had tried his best to look after her, often losing sleep because she needed so much of his attention through the night.

Sarah Lacey, who had rented a property from Samuel Cook for four years, told the inquest that just a few days before the tragedy, she had visited the Cooks at home to buy potatoes. Edith had bent over to weigh the potatoes and been unable to straighten up due to an intense pain in her thigh. Sarah told the inquest that Samuel had been kindness personified, putting his arms around Edith and helping her to get up. Sarah had spent two hours at the Cooks' home that evening and related that, while Samuel had been his normal self, Edith had been argumentative.

'Sam has broken a jug and I believe he did it on purpose,' Edith told Sarah.

'Why do ye tell these wilful lies, Edy?' Samuel asked her. 'You know I didn't do it on purpose.'

'Thee did'st, thee did'st,' argued Edith, who was poking the fire at the time. She suddenly rounded on her brother and aimed a blow at his head, although fortunately she missed and the poker connected with Samuel's hand. Samuel made no complaint about the blow and Sarah told the inquest that she believed that was because he was a shy man and was ashamed that Edith had behaved that way in front of a visitor to the house.

Another tenant, Elizabeth Fry, had visited the Cooks on the day before their deaths to pay her rent. She found Edith sitting in her chair by the fireside, in too much pain to move. Edith told Elizabeth that she had been in pain all night and that her brother had scarcely got a wink of sleep because he was in and out of bed looking after her. 'I begged him like an angel to bide in bed,' Edith said but Samuel had insisted on getting up time and time again to attend to his sister's needs and, as a result, was now feeling 'poorly'. Edith went on to say that Samuel wanted to call in Mr Biggs to treat her but she was afraid that the surgeon would blister her leg and she couldn't bear the pain. Elizabeth Fry suggested using a poultice of herbs and Samuel immediately went out to gather the ingredients she mentioned. He then prepared them and Elizabeth applied them to Edith's hip.

Before she left the house, Elizabeth advised Samuel not to worry too much about Edith, telling him, 'Don't take on any trouble like that, about what you can't help.'

'I cannot help but trouble,' Samuel replied.

Elizabeth finished her testimony by telling the coroner that Samuel always let Edith have her own way but that Edith never stopped arguing with him. 'He could not speak right,' Elizabeth stated.

William Wills was the next witness. He had been asked by Samuel to purchase some timber on his behalf and he also called at the cottage on the day before the deaths to discuss the price of the wood with Samuel. Seeing Edith in the garden, he asked her to pass a message to Samuel. 'What good is it to tell a crazy man?' Edith asked. 'I'm afraid to bide in the house with him, for he said he would kill me.'

The coroner took issue with the last few words of the conversation, telling Wills that he had never mentioned before the inquest that Samuel had threatened to kill his sister. Wills swore that he had but the coroner insisted that he hadn't, advising him to think carefully about his evidence. Wills then stated that Edith had been walking perfectly well and had not seemed to be in pain.

Samuel Cook's brother-in-law, Arthur Stone, told the inquest that since the death of his wife ten years earlier, Samuel had suffered from 'a low, weak mind' and that he was '... in a state of darkness.' According to Stone, Samuel was frequently 'much oppressed in spirit' and much given to sighing and groaning. At this, surgeon Mr Biggs was recalled to give his opinion on Samuel's state of mind.

Biggs told the inquest that while despondency could very well lead to suicide it was unlikely to lead to murder. 'A man in a low, nervous state would not be so likely to commit a murder as a man in a more violent state of monomania,' stated Biggs.

A member of the coroner's jury then raised the prevalent rumour that had spread around the area since the murder. There had been talk that Edith had been pregnant at the time of her death, carrying a child that had resulted from an incestuous relationship with her brother. Had this been investigated, asked the juror? Since Edith was in her late forties at the time of her death, this outrageous rumour was quickly quashed.

Having heard all the evidence, the coroner's jury retired. It took around three hours of deliberation for them to consider their verdict and, even then, they were unable to reach agreement.

In the case of Edith, the coroner's jury found a verdict of wilful murder against Samuel Cook. However, while they felt that Samuel Cook had committed suicide, they were unable to agree on the state of his mind at the time. The coroner therefore had no choice but to adjourn the inquest *sine die* – in other words, indefinitely. Thus it would be left for the judge at the next assizes to decide what was to be done about Samuel Cook.

Because of the verdict of the coroner's jury, Samuel Cook could not even be buried without permission from the judges. However, on 4 May 1842, it was reported in *The Times* that Cook's body had been secretly removed from his late residence and '... conveyed no one knows where, or by whom, or for what purpose.' Cook's neighbours were tight-lipped about the mysterious disappearance of his body. 'That the door was found open in the morning and the body gone is all that the neighbours know about the matter,' concluded the article.

4

'I'VE A GOOD MIND TO SERVE YOU THE SAME WAY'

St Philip's, 1846

On Sunday, 1 November 1846, Inspector Henry P. Webb was sitting in the charge room at St Philip's police station when he heard a horse-drawn vehicle pull up outside. Moments later, a young woman rushed into the police station.

Obviously drunk, the woman ran to where the inspector was sitting, seizing his arm. 'Oh, Mr Webb, you must take me into custody,' she said frantically and, when Webb asked her why, she told him that she had cut a man's throat.

Faced with a woman who was undoubtedly very tipsy and, going by his first impressions, quite possibly mad, Webb pressed her for more details. The near hysterical woman continued to insist that the inspector go to her house to see the man. Sergeant Franklyn, who was then in another room at the police station, heard the woman's desperate pleas and, to his mounting horror, he realised that he recognised her voice. He walked hurriedly into the front office to confirm his suspicions – the woman was his stepdaughter, Louisa Ferris.

Franklyn tried to get Louisa to calm down so that he and the inspector could establish what the problem was but she was practically incoherent. 'That man has disgraced me. And you,' Louisa shouted at him.

Realising that they were going to get very little sense out of Louisa, Franklyn and Inspector Webb set off to her house to see for themselves exactly who had disgraced who and with what outcome. However, they had not gone far before they were informed that a man had indeed been killed at Louisa's home in Lion Street and that the dead man was a fellow police officer, Patrick White. Hearing this, Webb and Franklyn went straight back to the police station, where they arrested Louisa Ferris and also her brother, James Edwards, who had driven her there. With the supposed murderess safely in custody, Webb and Franklyn went to her house in Lion Street.

By the time they arrived, the street outside Louisa's house was crowded with people and there were already two police constables there, trying to control between fifty or sixty interested spectators. There were large spots of blood on the pavement in front of the house and, as Webb and Franklyn went inside, it was immediately evident that someone had bled very heavily within its walls. In the sitting room, there were two sizeable pools of blood on the floor and yet more on the seat and back of a chair and on the walls. Webb and Franklyn were shown into another downstairs room, where a man lay dead on a bedstead. His clothes were drenched in blood, which had evidently poured from a deep gash on the right-hand side of the front of his throat.

As the police began to interview the people milling around the house, they gradually pieced together the series of events that had led to the untimely death of the thirty-seven-year-old Irish policeman.

It emerged that Louisa Ferris was a married woman, who, by mutual agreement, was separated from her husband, William. Since his departure to live near Chepstow, Louisa had taken in lodgers in order to support herself and her two children and, in November 1846, there were at least three sharing her house – William Stone, Elizabeth Jones and Patrick White.

White apparently found Louisa very attractive and had tried every trick in the book to persuade her into his bed, making what the contemporary newspapers referred to as 'overtures of an improper nature' towards her. When Louisa continued to refuse his advances, he plied her with 'drugged liquors' and so 'accomplished her ruin'. Almost inevitably, Louisa became pregnant and, fearful of the resultant scandal, White procured an abortion for her.

The day of the murder was Louisa's twenty-ninth birthday and she had persuaded her brother, James, to come and visit her. James arrived with a friend, Charles Sainsbury, and the two men were invited into the house, where they joined Louisa and Elizabeth and began chatting. It being a birthday celebration, there was plenty of drink flowing in the house and, by the time James and Charles arrived, Louisa had been drinking rum and at least two quarts of beer had been consumed. After a few minutes, Patrick White came into the room and sent Elizabeth out to buy another quart of beer.

Although Patrick White had drunk very little, he had plied both Louisa and Elizabeth Jones with alcohol and Elizabeth wasn't used to the effects of strong drink. Almost as soon as she had fetched the beer, she excused herself from the party and went to her room to lie down, falling into a deep sleep almost as soon as her head touched the pillow.

Before long, Elizabeth awoke with a start to find Patrick White standing at the side of her bed. She had just enough time to register the presence of Louisa Ferris in the bedroom doorway before Louisa stormed off downstairs.

She burst into the sitting room in a fury. 'Oh, that wretch,' she exclaimed. 'Is this your promise? They are both on the bed together,' she informed her other visitors, before leaving the room again, just as White entered. He calmly sat down and began to pour himself another glass of beer but, seconds later, Louisa came back. 'You nasty wretch,' she addressed White. 'Is this your promise?' she repeated. White said nothing but, as he bent forward to place his beer glass down, Louisa leaned towards him as if she were going to speak to him and her hand suddenly moved towards his throat. She made one quick slashing movement then ran out of the room again.

Nobody had seen anything in her hand and the first inkling that anyone had that there was anything wrong was when they heard the sound of blood spurting onto the floor. Charles Sainsbury immediately bolted out of the house through the back door like a startled rabbit, leaving James Edwards alone with White, who was gradually slumping forward in his chair.

Edwards rushed to support White but the injured man fought him, falling on his hands and knees to the floor and beginning to crawl out of the house. James followed him into the street, noticing as he did that people were beginning to hurry from the neighbouring houses to White's assistance.

Meanwhile, Elizabeth Jones had come downstairs to see what was happening. She met a furious Louisa at the bottom of the stairs who told her, 'I've a good mind to serve you the same way.' Elizabeth saw Louisa's hand move towards her and, ducking underneath her arm, ran straight out through the front door to the house next door. When she got there, she realised that her own throat was bleeding, although thankfully only from a very minor wound.

With Patrick White slowly bleeding to death on the street, Louisa flounced out of the house and demanded that James drive her to the police station in his horse-drawn fly. James looked across at White and saw that he was now being taken care of by a passerby, who was holding a handkerchief to the injured man's throat to try and staunch the bleeding. Realising that he could do little to help White, James did as his sister asked, dropping her off outside the police station then going to find their mother who, as well as being married to Sergeant Franklyn, was housekeeper at the police station.

Back in Lion Street, Richard Griffiths was still tending to Patrick White, who seemed desperate to talk to him. Eventually Griffiths held the edges of White's gaping wound together, allowing the injured man to speak. 'Mrs Ferris has cut my throat. Pray for me,' White said weakly.

'Pray yourself my good fellow. We cannot do you any good,' Griffiths advised him and White took him at his word.

'Lord have mercy on my soul,' he repeated three times, before falling back onto the pillow that someone had placed on the street for him. Within seconds, his eyes closed and he drew a couple of shuddering breaths and died 'all in a gore of blood'. Together the attending police officers and some of the neighbours carried him into his lodgings, which were then thoroughly searched. Before long, a bloodstained razor was found, which was obviously the murder weapon since there were several short, curly hairs still attached to it, similar to a man's beard hairs.

By the time the police surgeon Charles Joseph Hanson arrived at Lion Street, Patrick White had been dead for some time. However, when Hanson later conducted a post-mortem examination on White, he was certain that, even had he been with White at the very moment his throat was cut, the wound was so severe that he could not possibly have saved him. There was a single deep cut across White's throat, which was nearly four and a half inches long and had almost severed his head from his body, dividing both his windpipe and his jugular vein. White had died from a combination of blood loss and suffocation, as the blood from his throat entered his lungs and prevented him from breathing. Hanson believed that White could possibly have inflicted the wound himself, but it was so deep that he felt that it was highly unlikely. Interestingly, although White had otherwise been in good health, his liver had all the appearances of belonging to a person who was addicted to drink and, although it was not yet sufficiently damaged to kill him, Hanson believed that it would ultimately have done so.

An inquest was opened into the death of Patrick White at the New Inn on Lawford's Gate, before coroner Mr J.B. Grindon. Louisa Ferris was present at the inquest and sobbed bitterly as the succession of witnesses gave their evidence, occasionally burying her face in her hands. So great was her distress that Grindon gave her the option of leaving the hearing, an offer that she gratefully accepted. Thus, she was not present to hear the coroner's jury record a verdict of wilful murder against her.

Louisa Ferris appeared at the Gloucestershire Assizes before Mr Justice Gaselee in April 1847, with Mr Skinner and Mr Huddlestone prosecuting and Mr Keating acting in her defence.

By the time the case came to trial, there had already been extensive newspaper coverage of the murder, in which Louisa Ferris was largely portrayed as a victim rather than as a brutal murderess. She had married her husband when she was just sixteen years old and had borne him three children, one of whom had died in infancy. Although the couple had parted, the newspapers were quick to champion Louisa, stating that the separation did not arise due to any misconduct on her part.

She had taken in lodgers in order to support herself and her two surviving children and the newspapers described it as 'an evil hour' when Patrick White went to lodge with her. Much was made of his alleged seduction of her and the fact that he had apparently resorted to drugging her drinks in order to bed her, forcing her to have an abortion after she became pregnant. 'What his motive could have been in plying two women with drink on the day of his murder and, contrary to his habit, abstaining from it himself, can only be inferred,' wrote the reporter from the *Bristol Mercury*, casting a further slur on White's character.

Thus there was a considerable amount of public sympathy for Louisa Ferris, which, coupled with an impassioned speech by her defence counsel and a feeling

among the jury that there had been a considerable amount of provocation by White, resulted in a verdict of 'Guilty of manslaughter'.

Mr Justice Gaselee addressed Louisa before passing sentence, telling her:

> The jury have taken a very humane view of your case ... if they had found you guilty of murder your life would have been forfeited. You have had a very narrow escape. You have been found guilty of killing a person with whom you had been living in adultery. It shows the dreadful course of vice leading from one crime to another. It is necessary to make a severe example of you; human life has been sacrificed, probably without premeditation on your part and no doubt causing you much regret. You have given way to a dreadful passion; you have sent him, without time for repentance, to answer for his crimes before his Maker. You will have time – and probably a long time, by mercy of the jury – for repentance but you must repent in a foreign land, never more to return.

'Do not banish me, my Lord, from my poor children,' Louisa begged but the judge continued, regardless of her evident distress:

> You have had a narrow – a very narrow – escape and cannot be allowed to remain in this country. The sentence of this court is that you be transported beyond the seas to such place as her Majesty, by the advice of her privy council, shall direct, for the term of your natural life.

Louisa Ferris was transported to Van Diemen's Land, where she was a model prisoner. Indeed, her conduct was so exemplary that, by 1852, she had been granted a ticket of leave. However, having gained her freedom from prison, she almost immediately cut another man's throat in Melbourne, Australia. This time, she did not have a narrow escape.

5

'GOD FORGIVE THE MAN WHO DID IT'

Welsh Back, 1862

The young man swaggering down Welsh Back in the early hours of the morning of Sunday, 24 August 1862 was clearly drunk and apparently spoiling for a fight. When he met prostitute Jane Beer, he playfully seized her skirts and whipped them up over her head. Jane was not amused and remonstrated with her tormentor, telling him that he should be ashamed of himself. The man began to swear loudly at her, at which point a uniformed police constable was drawn to the scene by the sound of shouting and politely asked the young man to go home.

The man took little notice of PC 176, Christopher Wickham, who warned him again about his unseemly conduct and bad language, telling him that if he didn't go home, he would find himself taken to the police station. The young man staggered a few steps before stopping and defiantly telling the policeman, 'I will when I like.' He then gave PC Wickham a shove and Wickham retaliated in kind, sending him sprawling to the ground. He seized the young man firmly by the collar, hauled him to his feet and began to forcibly propel him towards the Bristol Bridge. The man protested that his home was in the opposite direction, at which Wickham let him go and told him to go anywhere he liked as long as he went away. He warned the man that he would be back in a few minutes to check that he had left the area and that this was his last warning – either he went home quietly or he would be arrested.

Wickham would happily have left the young man to go home and sleep off his excesses, providing he caused no more trouble, but the man was having none of it. When Wickham returned to the area a few minutes later, he was waiting for him, demanding that the officer escort him back to his home in King Street so that he could prove that he lived there. He was so insistent that Wickham's patience finally snapped and he placed his hand on the young man's shoulder and told him that he was under arrest.

The young man immediately began to kick out at PC Wickham's shins, shouting, 'You ******* swine. If you don't let me go I will strike you.' Almost as soon as the words were out of his mouth, Wickham suddenly released his hold on the young man and raised his hand towards his own head.

'I'm stabbed. I'm stabbed,' he said in surprise and shock, running off in the direction of the Bristol Royal Infirmary.

The affray had been witnessed by a number of bystanders, one of whom knew both PC Wickham and his attacker very well. Samuel Bryant went off in search of another policeman, while another bystander, William Ferris, took hold of the young man and attempted to detain him. However, the man broke free from his grasp and ran off towards his home and by the time Bryant returned with PC John Parsons, there was nothing to be seen but a few large drops of blood on the footpath.

Fortunately, Bryant was able to identify the drunken young man as Bristol and Exeter Railway labourer Robert Morgan, who lived at 2 King Street. Accompanied by Bryant and Ferris, PC Parsons immediately went to the address, which was divided into a number of apartments. The front door of the house wasn't locked and, as the three men entered, they could hear somebody moving about in one of the upstairs rooms. When they went to investigate, they found Morgan undressed and lying on his bed, either sound asleep or pretending to be.

Parsons asked Ferris if he was absolutely sure that this was the man he had seen fighting with PC Wickham and, when Ferris swore that it was, Parsons took Morgan's arm and told him that he was under arrest for stabbing a police constable on the Welsh Back. Morgan made no attempt to deny the charge. After a few moments of silence he said resignedly, 'I shall trust in providence. There is a God above.' He was then instructed to dress before being escorted to the police station.

View from the Welsh Back. (Author's collection)

Welsh Back, 2010. (© N. Sly)

Parsons searched Morgan's clothes before allowing him to put them on and also made a quick search of his room but found no weapon. It was only when Morgan arrived at the police station and was searched again that a small pocket knife was found hidden in the lining of his waistcoat. The knife was folded closed and, when Parsons opened it, he saw that it still glistened with fresh blood.

Meanwhile, PC Wickham had made his own way to the Bristol Royal Infirmary, where it was found that he had a three or four-inch long wound just below his left ear. It appeared to have been made by a small but sharp knife, which had been plunged into his neck and then pulled upwards, severing both the carotid and vertebral arteries and causing a massive haemorrhage. Although Wickham was still conscious and able to talk coherently, he was weak through loss of blood and fainted twice as he tried to explain what had happened to him.

Initially, the hospital doctors were confident that Wickham's injury would not prove fatal. However, a few days later, he began to bleed again and although the doctors applied pressure to the wound, it took some time for the bleeding to stop.

Because of the seriousness of Wickham's condition, it was now decided to take his deposition and accordingly, on 31 August, magistrate William Herepath was summoned to the hospital along with his clerk, John Frederick Williams. In the presence of Robert Morgan, Wickham dictated his statement to Williams, who wrote it down as he spoke.

Having positively identified Morgan as the man with whom he had scuffled on Welsh Back a week earlier, Wickham went on to describe the exchange of words between them and his repeated requests for Morgan to go home quietly. He then deposed that he had been stabbed in the neck, although he admitted that there were a lot of other people around at the time and that consequently he didn't know who had stabbed him. 'The prisoner was the only person I had any altercation with,' added Wickham, who then told the magistrate that he had been in great pain since his admission to hospital and felt very weak and ill, so much so that he truly believed that he was going to die.

Robert Morgan was offered the opportunity to question PC Wickham but declined to do so, saying, 'I have no question to ask him.' The deposition was then read aloud to Wickham, who signed it with his cross as a true record.

In the event, Christopher Wickham lingered in hospital until 25 September before he finally succumbed to the repeated blood loss occasioned by his wound. Almost his last words were, 'God forgive the man who did it'; followed by an assurance to the doctors that he personally had forgiven Morgan.

An inquest was opened at the hospital by coroner Mr J.B. Grindon. Assistant house surgeon Dr Broad, who had treated PC Wickham in hospital and subsequently performed a post-mortem examination, told the inquest that Wickham had died due to excessive haemorrhage, following prolonged internal bleeding from the wound in his neck. Once Broad's evidence had been heard, the inquest was adjourned since one of the key witnesses was away from Bristol.

King Street. (Author's collection)

Welsh Back, 2010. (© N. Sly)

When the proceedings re-opened, the main witnesses were Jane Beer, Samuel Bryant and William Ferris, all of whom had witnessed the altercation between Wickham and Robert Morgan. All admitted that there had been a number of people milling about at the time and none of them had actually seen Robert Morgan stab Wickham.

Indeed, only one person claimed to have witnessed the stabbing. Confectioner James Jones told the inquest that he had clearly seen Morgan pull a knife from his waistcoat pocket and stab Wickham once in the left-hand side of his neck. Jones stated that Wickham had immediately cried out 'I'm stabbed', after which he slumped against the wall of the Prince's Head public house. Jones said that he had applied his handkerchief to the wound on Wickham's neck and then supported him to the High Street, where he had handed him over to another policeman.

Samuel Bryant interrupted Jones's statement to tell the jury, 'He wasn't near the spot, gentlemen.' When Grindon reprimanded Bryant, telling him that he should address any remarks directly to the coroner, Bryant approached him.

'You have something to say?' Grindon asked him.

'Yes, sir, this man wasn't there at all,' replied Bryant.

Grindon turned to Jones and asked him if he was aware of the penalty for not telling the truth. Jones said that he was and insisted that he had given a truthful account.

With that, the coroner summarised the evidence for his jury, reminding them that although only Jones purported to have seen the fatal blow actually struck, other witnesses had seen Morgan's hand close to Wickham's head and, in spite of the crowd of bystanders, it was abundantly clear from their evidence that nobody else had been close enough to the officer to stab him. Since PC Wickham was clearly in police uniform and, at the time of the offence, was engaged in the just and honest execution of his duty, if the jury believed the evidence of the witnesses then their only possible verdict was one of wilful murder against Robert Morgan.

The jury needed only a short deliberation to come to the same conclusion and Morgan was committed for trial on the coroner's warrant at the next Gloucester Assizes. Twenty-five-year-old Morgan, who was known as a respectable, sober and hard-working man, was obviously horrified by his own actions and looked ill and anxious as he heard the decision of the inquest. His two sisters, who were present at the proceedings, burst into noisy sobs as he was led away to await his trial.

The proceedings opened before Mr Justice Mellor on 18 December 1862 with Mr Harrington and Mr Cooke prosecuting the case and Mr Cripps acting in defence of Morgan.

Mr Cooke began by describing the events of 24 August, pointing out to the jury that a serving police constable was entitled to special consideration and therefore what might otherwise be considered manslaughter in the eyes of the law was nothing less than murder when the victim was an officer killed in the execution of his duty. Thus, if the jury were satisfied by the evidence they were about to hear and found the prisoner guilty of wilfully inflicting the injury that ultimately proved fatal to PC Wickham, then the only possible verdict open to them was one of wilful murder.

The first witnesses to be called were the doctors who had treated PC Wickham during his stay in hospital. The first of these, Mr Augustin Prichard, described Wickham's injury, explaining that although the wound in his neck was stitched and had healed externally, the internal arterial bleeding had continued, in spite of the surgeons' best efforts to stop it. Although the doctors had eventually tied the carotid artery in an unsuccessful effort to stem Wickham's blood loss, they were unaware of the full extent of the damage to his vertebral artery, which was completely inaccessible to them while he was still alive and was thus only discovered at his post-mortem examination. Prichard's testimony was confirmed by Dr Edmund Comer Broad, after which the prosecution tried to introduce Wickham's deposition as evidence.

This initiated an immediate objection from the judge since, at the time it was taken, neither the magistrate nor his clerk had thought to include the offence with which the accused was charged in the heading. Robert Morgan was then in custody on a charge of cutting and wounding PC Wickham and Mr Justice Mellor believed that this information should rightfully have appeared on the actual deposition, arguing that it would have proved that the accused was fully aware of the charge against him and that he had been given the opportunity to ask any relevant questions of the victim pertaining to that charge.

Clerk Mr Williams argued that the section had deliberately been left blank because, at the time, nobody was sure what the defendant would ultimately be charged with, given that Wickham was making the deposition under the impression that he would not recover from his injuries. However, Mellor cited a recent case from the York Assizes in which the ruling by two eminent judges had been that some offence should always be stated on the deposition so that the accused might have the opportunity to cross-examine. With that ruling in mind, Mellor thought it best to exclude the deposition for the time being, although he was happy for it to be heard if the counsel for the defence specifically requested it. Not surprisingly, Mr Cripps declined the judge's offer.

The court then heard from Jane Beer, Samuel Bryant and William Ferris, who repeated the testimony they had already given at the inquest. However, Samuel Bryant now testified that he had seen Morgan strike PC Wickham in the neck rather than saying, as he had at the inquest, that he had merely witnessed a scuffle between the two men, in the course of which Wickham raised his hand to his head, saying, 'I'm stabbed'. (There is nothing in the contemporary newspaper coverage of the trial to suggest that James Jones was called as a witness.)

PC John Parsons related the arrest of Robert Morgan and the discovery of the knife in the lining of his waistcoat. Asked whether Morgan was inebriated at the time of his capture, Parsons stated that although Morgan might have been drinking, he could still walk without assistance and showed little sign of drunkenness.

Mr Cooke tried once more to have Wickham's deposition admitted as evidence but defence counsel Mr Cripps objected to its inclusion and, when the objection was sustained by the judge, Cooke rested his case, leaving Cripps to begin his defence of Robert Morgan.

Cripps began by describing Robert Morgan to the jury as an honest and industrious worker who lived with and supported his widowed mother and who was generally known for his quiet and orderly conduct. Prior to this 'unfortunate occurrence', he had never been in any trouble.

Cripps told the jury that he held out no hope that they would acquit his client, since the facts of the case had been clearly established before them. The utmost he could hope for was that the jury would find that the crime of which the prisoner was guilty was manslaughter rather than murder.

Ordinarily, a charge of wilful murder implied some malice aforethought on behalf of the accused, explained Cripps. Up to the moment of the stabbing of Christopher Wickham, there was no suggestion of any feelings of enmity, hatred or revenge between him and Morgan – indeed, the two were perfect strangers, whose paths had never crossed before.

Cripps then directed the jury's attention to the weapon, reminding them that it was not a dagger or even a cutting knife, but a tiny penknife. So small and insignificant was the knife that they had heard the surgeons say in court that a man might have struck fifty blows with it and not caused the amount of damage that had resulted from this one blow. This, said Cripps, was not a murderous attack but a chance blow, from which dreadful results had ensued.

It was dark at the time, continued Cripps, and his client admitted that he was drunk. Could the jury be sure that Morgan had been fully aware at the time that Wickham was a serving policeman in uniform? Was it not possible that Wickham had seen the young man as a habitual drunk and consequently been rough in his handling of him, provoking him into lashing out in order to free himself? And, in view of the darkness, could the jury rely on the evidence of those witnesses who had identified Morgan as Wickham's murderer?

Had the victim been a civilian rather than a serving police officer, this would surely have been a case of manslaughter, insisted Cripps. The death of PC Wickham was due to an unhappy chance blow rather than by murderous design and although the prisoner should receive long and grievous punishment as a consequence, he should not have to pay for this unfortunate act by forfeiting his life.

Finally, Cripps called two character witnesses for his client, both of whom described Morgan as quiet, inoffensive, hard-working and sober. One, Alfred Gibbons, stated that he had known Morgan for ten years and, in that time, had only twice seen him the worse for drink.

It was then left to the judge to summarise the evidence for the jury. He began by reminding them that this was not an ordinary case of murder but was actually the unlawful killing of a police officer whilst engaged in the execution of his duty. It was indisputable that a part of Wickham's duties was the apprehension of people who were disorderly in the street and the judge reminded the jury that Mr Cripps had agreed that Wickham was justified in apprehending Robert Morgan. Given the indecent assault on Jane Beer and Morgan's subsequent bad language and defiance, it appeared to Mellor that Wickham had shown a great deal of moderation, forbearance and propriety in his dealings with the prisoner. What the jury must determine was whether or not they believed that Wickham had used any unnecessary violence and also whether or not Morgan had been fully aware that Wickham was a policeman. Only if Morgan were not aware of Wickham's status could the crime be manslaughter – if the jury believed that Morgan recognised the true identity of his victim then they must find him guilty of murder.

Finally, the judge warned the jury not to be swayed by the fact that Morgan was his widowed mother's only son and her sole means of support. They had an obligation to society and should not allow themselves to be led by feelings of compassion. Mellor urged them to do their duty to the prisoner, the public and humanity manfully and conscientiously, whatever the result.

The jury retired for thirty minutes before returning to pronounce Robert Morgan 'Guilty' of the wilful murder of Christopher Wickham. However, as Mr Cripps had hoped, they unanimously recommended him to mercy.

'On what grounds is the recommendation to mercy based?' enquired the judge. 'Are there any special grounds other than compassion?'

Arno's Vale Cemetery. (Author's collection)

The foreman of the jury answered on behalf of his colleagues. The jury are not sure whether the prisoner actually knew he was a policeman or not.

Almost immediately, the foreman realised that they had been given specific instructions by the judge that, in the event of any such doubts, an appropriate verdict would have been manslaughter. As the judge began to ask, 'Am I to understand, gentlemen ... ?' the foreman quickly interrupted him.

'I had better retract that. It was that two witnesses bore testimony to his good character,' he said hastily.

With that, Mellor pronounced sentence of death on Robert Morgan, who was taken to Bristol Prison to await his execution.

Thirty-nine-year-old Christopher Wickham left a pregnant wife, who was about to give birth to the couple's seventh child. Immediately after the conclusion of the inquest, he was buried with full police honours at Arno's Vale Cemetery. The cost of the funeral was met by the Watch Committee, while a public fund was opened for the support of his widow and children, who were now destitute. Yet Maryann Wickham was one of the first of many to petition for a reprieve for her husband's killer. On 3 January 1863 it was reported that royal clemency had been extended towards Robert Morgan and that his sentence was to be commuted to one of penal servitude for life.

Morgan had not been informed of the efforts on his behalf until their final outcome was known. While in the condemned cell at Bristol Prison, his conduct had been irreproachable and he was described in the contemporary newspapers as having borne his fate with great fortitude and a placid, patient and trustful demeanour. He had continued to display his normal quiet, thoughtful character, while at the same time showing great remorse, sorrow and repentance for the act that he had committed.

Informed of his reprieve, Morgan was overcome by emotion and, having thanked all those who had exerted themselves on his behalf, he announced that he intended to ensure that his future life was an atonement for his past.

Note: Robert Morgan's age is variously given as twenty-five and twenty-seven years old at the time of the murder.

6

'I'LL KNOCK YOUR BLOODY SKULL IN!'

Hotwells, 1862

If there had been such a thing as an ASBO in the nineteenth century, Mary Ann French of Hotwell Road would probably have been first in the queue to receive one. She had several arrests for drunkenness to her name and, with a drink inside her, liked nothing more than to pick a fight with anyone who upset her.

In November 1857, she was seen near her home by a policeman, drunk and spoiling for a fight. She was persuaded to go indoors to sober up but quickly came out into the street again, now with a baby in her arms. Afraid that she might injure the child, the policeman arrested her and she found herself before the magistrates charged with being drunk and disorderly and with making use of indecent language.

Mary Ann's only defence on that occasion was to say that she was in the habit of getting drunk occasionally. If she could afford to find money to get drunk then she could afford to find money for the fine, said the magistrate, ordering her to pay five shillings.

In July of 1858, Mary Ann was again up before the magistrates on the same charge, although this time the magistrate was more lenient and let her off with a caution, on the grounds that her drunkenness had been aggravated by her husband's ill-treatment of her.

Mary Ann and her husband, Abraham, rented an upstairs apartment in a house in Hotwell Road, and sailor George Dyer and his wife, Alice, lived downstairs in another apartment in the same house. There was evidently bad blood between the two couples, since on 24 September 1862 there was a series of incidents that eventually led to the death of thirty-seven-year-old Alice Dyer and the trial of Mary Ann French for her murder.

The evening began with Mary Ann French drinking beer in the Oddfellows' Arms public house. Alice Dyer was also in the pub and apparently made a remark to which Mary Ann took objection. Before long, the two women were fighting, rolling around on the ground with Abraham French an interested spectator, egging his wife on from the sidelines. George Dyer arrived on the scene and he in turn began a violent altercation with Abraham French. By now, somebody had summoned the police, who managed to separate the combatants. Once the police had spoken to some of the bystanders at the fight, Mary Ann and Abraham French were marched off to the police station, while the Dyers were told to make their way home.

The Dyers fled to the home of their landlady and next-door neighbour, Mrs Ann King, who kept the Nightingale Tavern on Hotwell Road. Mary Ann Dyer was quickly released from custody and she and her husband followed the Dyers to Mrs King's and tried to force their way into her premises to get at them. Although Mrs King managed to thwart their attempts to get in and locked the door, Mary Ann and Abraham remained outside shouting at the Dyers for some time, threatening to 'beat their brains in' and 'raise a kernel on their nuts'. The commotion attracted the attention of two patrolling police constables, who took Mary Ann into custody again. Feeling that it was now safe to leave, George and Alice Dyer returned to their own apartment.

Susan Harris, who had witnessed the fight outside the pub, went to the police station with Mary Ann, who was only detained for a short while and then sent home again. Susan went back to her house with her and was sitting in the upstairs apartment with Mary Ann and Abraham. They had not been home for more than fifteen minutes when Mary Ann abruptly left the room, carrying a lighted candle. Almost immediately, there was the noise of a scuffle downstairs and, when Susan went to see what was happening, she found Mary Ann arguing with the Dyers. Soon, Abraham French came downstairs and, before long, he and George Dyer were throwing punches at each other again.

Hotwells. (Author's collection)

As the two men fought, Mary Ann called for her daughter to fetch a 'flat' from her room (Mary Ann worked as an ironer and so possessed a number of flat irons). She repeated the request several times before the child actually fetched the iron and handed it to her mother, who promptly hit Alice Dyer over the head with it.

Alice Dyer staggered back to her room, blood pouring from her head and running down her neck. Susan Harris went with her and tried to bathe the wound but it was bleeding so heavily that it took three pails of water to wash away the blood. Susan suggested cutting Alice's hair and applying a sticking plaster to the injury but Alice wouldn't allow her to do that, saying that her head hurt far too much to be able to bear having a plaster on it. Eventually, Susan wrapped Alice's head in a towel and the flow of blood gradually slowed and stopped.

Minutes later, as Susan Harris sat with Alice and George Dyer in their apartment, there was a tremendous crash as Mary Ann French burst through the locked door wielding a poker. Before anyone could stop her, she rushed at Alice Dyer without speaking and hit her hard on the back of the head. Alice Dyer fell to the ground at which Mary Ann shouted, 'I'll knock your bloody skull in!' before running out of the apartment. She remained on the landing for some time shouting threats at the Dyers. The police were summoned again and Mary Ann was taken into custody, having first been relieved of her poker.

Alice Dyer regained consciousness and was put to bed. However, the next morning, she was still feeling the effects of the previous night's shenanigans and walked to the Clifton Dispensary for some treatment. By 5 October, her condition had worsened rather than improved, so she walked to the Bristol Royal Infirmary. She was examined by house surgeon Mr Edmund Comer Broad, who immediately admitted her for treatment as an in-patient.

It was obvious to Broad that Alice Dyer was seriously ill. Not only was she still suffering from the effects of the injury to her head but she had also developed tetanus. In spite of receiving treatment for both conditions, Alice Dyer died on the evening of 6 October. She remained conscious and sensible almost to the last, sending for the hospital chaplain less than two hours before her eventual death.

Mr Broad conducted a post-mortem examination the next day. He discovered a wound on the left-hand side of the back of Alice's head which was rather curiously shaped like the letter X with one 'leg' missing. Broad believed that the injury was most probably caused either by a blow with a poker, or from a stick with a knob on the end of it, or by the deceased banging the back of her head on the ground. He couldn't completely discount a fall or a blow from a fist as having caused the injury but strongly felt that a blow from a blunt instrument was the most likely contender. He determined the cause of Alice Dyer's death as tetanus, arising from the wound on her head.

Broad was the first person to speak at the inquest into Alice Dyer's death, opened at the infirmary by coroner Mr J.B. Grindon. He was followed by George Dyer, Susan Harris and Mrs King and, once they had given their accounts of the events of 24 September, the coroner ordered the arrest of Abraham French, who was present at the proceedings.

PC Henry Drake told the inquest of arresting Mary Ann French, saying that she still had a poker in her hand when she was detained for the last time. Both PC Drake and Mrs King stated that, during the earlier fight with Alice Dyer, Mary Ann French had been banging Alice's head against the pavement.

Bristol Royal Infirmary. (Author's collection)

Several eyewitnesses to the various fights then testified. One, Robert Philpott, who lived on Hotwell Road, believed that Mrs King had been inciting the Dyers. Another resident of Hotwell Road, tailor Jonathan Price, insisted that after Mary Ann was arrested for the second time, George Dyer challenged Abraham French to a fight in the street. Overall, the witnesses painted a confusing picture for the inquest jury, with each claiming to have seen different things at different times.

Once all of the eyewitnesses had been heard, the nurse who had cared for Alice in hospital testified, followed by Alice's sister. Mary Ann French then asked if she might make a statement.

When the coroner agreed, Mary Ann said that she had been having a quiet drink in the Oddfellows' Arms when Alice Dyer had insulted her. Telling the court that both the Dyers were 'pretty tipsy', Mary Ann admitted that there had been a fight. However, she insisted that she had not struck Alice Dyer's head against the pavement – on the contrary, Alice Dyer had assaulted her, ripping a sizeable hank of hair from the back of her head. Once they were all back at home, Alice Dyer had insulted Mary Ann and her daughter. Mary Ann admitted to threatening to hit Alice with a flat but swore that she had not actually carried out her threat. Finally, Mary Ann maintained that she herself had called a policeman to try and stop the Dyers from fighting but that the constable had refused to intervene, saying that he saw no need to do so.

After some deliberation, the coroner's jury returned a verdict of manslaughter against Mary Ann French. No evidence was found against Abraham French, who was released from custody at the termination of the inquest. However, even though the inquest had reached a verdict of manslaughter against Mary Ann French, she still had go before the magistrates, who determined that she should stand trial for the more serious charge of wilful murder.

Hotwells and Cumberland Basin, 1928. (Author's collection)

Thus it was on a charge of wilful murder that Mary Ann was tried at the Gloucester Winter Assizes before Mr Justice Mellor. (She appeared at the same assizes as the killer of PC Christopher Wickham, as described in Chapter Five.)

The case was prosecuted by Mr Cooke and, when Mr Justice Mellor found out that Mary Ann had no defence counsel, he asked Mr Sawyer to act on her behalf. Mary Ann bemoaned the fact that her trial was not taking place in Bristol, saying that, if it had been, she could have produced numerous witnesses to her innocence.

Mr Cooke opened the proceedings by reviewing the events on the evening of 24 September, telling the jury that it was beyond all doubt that Mary Ann had killed Alice Dyer. The question for the jury to decide would be whether or not she had committed the offence with malice aforethought. If they believed that she had, it would be their duty to find her guilty of wilful murder but, on the other hand, if they felt that Mary Ann had been provoked and reacted to that provocation in a passion, then the correct verdict would be one of manslaughter.

Mr Cooke then called the witnesses for the prosecution, who all gave precisely the same testimony as they had already given before the coroner and magistrates. Yet, in court, the witnesses were asked to provide more detail about the drunkenness or otherwise of the main protagonists in the case and to say whether or not they believed that Mary Ann had acted in passion.

Susan Harris admitted that Mary Ann 'had had a drop to drink'.

'A drop means a good deal in Bristol,' clarified Mr Cooke.

'She was in a great passion,' remarked the judge and Susan Harris agreed with him that she was.

The judge repeated his remark to Ann King after she had testified and Ann – who had just spoken about the repeated violence and threats exhibited by Mary Ann and Abraham French towards the Dyers – pointedly agreed that 'She was in her usual passion.'

The court then heard from surgeon Mr Broad about his treatment of Alice Dyer in hospital and the subsequent post-mortem examination. Although he still gave tetanus as the ultimate cause of Alice Dyer's death, Broad was now prepared to say that the injury to her head was also sufficiently serious that it might have caused her demise. He also stated that he could not rule out a bang on the head from a fall as having caused Alice's injury, although he firmly believed that the injury had been made by a blunt instrument with some kind of knob on the end, such as the poker that Mary Ann French had been brandishing on her arrest.

Having only agreed that morning to act as defence counsel, Mr Sawyer was at somewhat of a disadvantage when it came to his closing speech. However, he made a brave effort on behalf of his client, asking the jury to find her guilty of manslaughter rather than murder and saying that the evidence they had heard in court could only sustain the lesser charge.

Mr Justice Mellor then summarised the case for the jury. He began by reminding them that the coroner's jury had found a verdict of manslaughter against Mary Ann French. He advised the jury to completely disregard this verdict, telling them that they had no way of knowing exactly what had occurred at the inquest to merit such a decision. Mellor said that he could not argue with the verdict from the inquest, but then again, neither could he argue with the conclusions of the magistrates, who had committed the defendant on a charge of wilful murder. Thus, it was for the jury to consider the case with open minds, arriving at their verdict only on the evidence they had heard that day in court. If they were not satisfied that the blow with the poker caused Alice Dyer's death, they should give the defendant the benefit of that doubt.

The key to the case, said Mellor, was provocation. If the jury were of the opinion that the defendant inflicted the blow with the intention of causing grievous bodily harm, they should find her guilty of wilful murder. On the other hand, if the jury felt that there had been reasonable provocation prior to the striking of the blow that caused the victim's death, the correct verdict would be one of manslaughter. However, for a verdict of manslaughter, the provocation must have occurred immediately before the blow was struck, without an interval during which they might have expected the defendant's blood to cool and reason prevail.

The jury needed only a brief period of deliberation before agreeing on the lesser of the two charges, finding Mary Ann French 'Guilty of manslaughter'.

Mr Justice Mellor addressed Mary Ann French telling her that, while he could not argue with the jury's verdict, he sincerely believed that they had viewed her case most mercifully and that he personally believed very strongly that her crime was murder. She had hit her victim with an instrument calculated 'to do the most serious mischief' and she had done so after sufficient time had elapsed for her anger to cool after the previous brawl.

Mellor told Mary Ann that he found it sad that she had been reduced to circumstances that had almost led to the forfeit of her life. It was a most dreadful thing for her to have been living in the way described by the witnesses – drinking, brawling, brandishing pokers and using violent and abominable language. The seriousness of her offence demanded a serious punishment, said Mellor, sentencing thirty-five-year-old Mary Ann French to fifteen years of penal servitude.

Mary Ann was horrified at the severity of her sentence. 'Oh, my dear man! Oh, my dear judge!' she exclaimed, before being removed from the dock, her cries for mercy echoing through the court for some minutes after she had left the room.

Mary Ann French served the majority of her sentence at the Female Convict Prison in Knaphill in Surrey. It appears that, on her release, she returned to live with Abraham in Hotwell Road – although most probably not in premises owned by Mrs King.

Note: There are two different dates given in the contemporary newspapers for Alice Dyer's death – 6 and 8 October.

7

'I WOULD RATHER DIE THAN GO TO GAOL'

Bedminster, 1867

Thirty-seven-year-old Susanna Maggs of Charlotte Street in Bedminster was in deep trouble. Her husband, George, who worked as a labourer for the Bristol Local Board of Health, was ill and could only work sporadically to support his wife and three children, so Susanna took in washing to supplement his earnings of fifteen shillings a week. However, according to the contemporary newspapers, by 1867 Susanna had become 'irregular and improvident in her habits'. Unbeknown to George, she began to dip into the rent money and also to pawn some of the garments that she was given to launder. Not surprisingly, the rightful owners of these items demanded their return and threatened to go to the police.

Susanna was known to suffer from depression and when she threatened to commit suicide, her friends and family took little notice, having heard her make similar threats many times before. This time, however, Susanna seemed more determined than ever before, telling her lodger, Mrs Dennis on 27 May, 'I would rather die than go to gaol.'

Mrs Dennis didn't take her seriously, even when Susanna later told her that she had purchased poison. 'Perhaps before this time tomorrow I may be laid a corpse and the child with me,' she said, referring to her youngest daughter, sixteen-month-old Susan. What nobody knew was that Susanna had spent the day visiting chemist's and druggist's shops, purchasing opium on the pretext of wanting to make some cough mixture.

Mrs Dennis saw Susanna again on Sunday 28 May and was later to describe her mood as very sullen, bad tempered and vexed, saying that she looked 'very wild and ghastly about the eyes.' Susanna continued to complain bitterly about her troubled life and to threaten to end it but, once again, nobody believed that she would actually carry out her threats. However, in the early hours of the morning of Monday 29 May, Susanna woke her husband and wished him 'Goodbye'.

George asked her what she meant, at which Susanna confessed to having poisoned herself and their infant daughter with opium. At first, George didn't believe her but one glance at baby Susan convinced him of the awful truth. In desperation, he called Mrs Dennis to help. Mrs Dennis found Susanna in bed with baby Susan at her breast. Apparently unable to move her limbs, Susanna asked her lodger to lift the child from her arms, saying that she had taken 'something' and given the baby some as well.

Susan was rushed unconscious and unresponsive to the Bristol General Hospital, where she was surrendered to the care of house surgeon Mr Siddall and his staff. The doctors fought valiantly to save her life but sadly she succumbed to the effects of the poison administered by her mother and died the following Tuesday morning. Meanwhile, the police were summoned to the house on Charlotte Street to deal with Susanna.

When the first policeman arrived, he found that Susanna was very drowsy, although still capable of walking and of talking rationally. She too was taken to hospital and, unlike her daughter, responded well to treatment. Naturally, Mr Siddall was anxious to know exactly what she had given Susan and Susanna informed him that she had dissolved a pea-sized piece of opium in a pan with some sugar and water and then fed the liquid to the baby, after which she had taken a similar dose herself. 'You don't know my troubles. They are very great,' she told Mr Siddall tearfully, adding that she had intended to destroy herself but was afraid that her husband did not have long to live and, fearing what might happen to her baby when she was left an orphan, had decided to take her daughter with her.

Mr Siddall estimated that a pea-sized lump of opium would weigh four or five grains, a more than fatal dose for so young a child. He conducted a post-mortem examination on the baby and concluded that Susan was an otherwise perfectly healthy child, who had died from the effects of a narcotic poison. When Susanna's home was searched, a jug containing the residue of the sugar and opium mixture that she had admitted to feeding to her baby was found.

An inquest was opened into Susan's death at the Wagon and Horses Inn on Redcliff Hill by deputy coroner Mr H.S. Wasbrough. Having heard the medical evidence and the testimony of Mrs Dennis, Mr Wasbrough addressed the inquest jury.

He told them that it was their job to determine whether Susan Maggs had died as a result of the ingestion of poison and, if they were of the opinion that she had, whether this poison was administered by the child's mother or anyone else and finally whether it had been given with the intention and purpose of destroying life. Wasbrough told the jury that the medical evidence seemed to clearly indicate that Susan Maggs had been poisoned and that the presumption of guilt was very strong against her mother.

He pointed out that there could be questions for a higher tribunal on Susanna's sanity and it might ultimately be shown that she was of unsound mind. However, such questions could not be considered at the inquest and it was therefore the duty of the jury to answer just two questions – did Susan Maggs die by poison and, if so, was that poison given to her by her mother for the purpose of causing her death.

If the jury answered yes to both questions, then their only possible verdict was one of wilful murder against Susanna Maggs. The jury deliberated briefly before informing the coroner that they had unanimously agreed on this verdict.

Although still recovering from her attempted suicide, Susanna was committed for trial on the coroner's warrant and was eventually discharged from hospital straight to prison to await the start of the proceedings against her. Her trial opened at Bristol Assizes on 15 August 1867 before Mr Justice Willes. The case was prosecuted by Mr Saunders, while Mr Folkard and Mr St Aubyn conducted Susanna's defence.

The court first heard from Mrs Dennis and surgeon Mr Siddall about the events leading up to the death of baby Susan. It was brought to the attention of the court that Susanna Maggs was still breastfeeding her daughter and Mr Siddall was questioned about whether or not this was unusual. Siddall informed the court that some mothers suckled their children until they were six or seven years old but added that nine or ten months was the most appropriate age for breastfeeding to cease.

The next witness to be called was Mrs Hamilton, a midwife who had attended Susanna Maggs at her daughter's birth. Susanna had borne five children, in each case experiencing a difficult labour and Susan's birth was the hardest of them all. Mrs Hamilton told the court that she had been back and forth to tend to Susanna for nine days and that, after the birth, Susanna had suffered from 'an overflow of milk to the head', a condition that would probably be recognised today as post-natal depression.

Although Susanna had not completely lost her senses, after each of her five confinements she was 'stupefied', suffering from intolerable pains in her head and 'a spasmodic affection of the brain'. She had also experienced hallucinations.

Mrs Hamilton had last seen Susanna Maggs on 7 May, when she was 'in a very low, melancholy state'. She was still complaining of excruciating pains in her head and was now suffering from what the midwife referred to as 'inward complaints'.

Once Mrs Hamilton had testified, defence counsel Mr Folkard addressed the court. He insisted that Susanna Maggs was a 'poor, unhappy woman', who was more deserving of pity and compassion than of the extreme punishment of the law. There was, in this sad and melancholy story, a complete absence of any malice aforethought. Susanna Maggs had been a fond and caring mother to all of her children, even though she had suffered severely at all her confinements with an overflow of milk to the head, which had produced a morbid and desponding state of mind.

It was for the jury to determine the state of Susanna's mind at the time of the murder, Folkard continued. A sane person had a motive for murder, he told them, while an insane person generally had no motive whatsoever. A sane person generally tried to conceal his or her crime but an insane person did not attempt any concealment. Sane persons usually killed those who were antagonistic towards them, whereas the insane frequently killed those who were dearest to them. Every bit of evidence submitted by the prosecution indicated sufficient proof of delusions and morbid feelings existing in his client's mind and this was more than enough to justify an acquittal by the jury on the grounds of Susanna's insanity.

Mr Justice Willes instructed the jury to determine whether or not Susan Maggs was poisoned with opium and, if so, if her mother administer that poison. If she did, Willes told the jury that it was up to them to decide on whether the most appropriate verdict was guilty of wilful murder, guilty of manslaughter or acquittal on the grounds of insanity. The judge then said that he could quite believe that a woman could be in such a morbid state of mind as to convince herself that what she was doing in removing her child from the world was actually beneficial for that child.

Throughout his summary of the evidence, Mr Justice Willes seemed to be hinting that the most appropriate verdict would be one of guilty of manslaughter and it was this verdict that the jury eventually plumped for, adding a rider that they felt that there were extenuating circumstances. Expressing his approval for the verdict, Willes nevertheless reminded Susanna Maggs that she had committed a very serious offence and ordered her to be kept in penal servitude for the next seven years.

The outcome of the trial caused an immediate public outcry, eloquently expressed in the *Pall Mall Gazette* of 19 August 1867. After a brief outline of the facts of the case, the paper went on to state:

> The judge's charge, the verdict and the subsequent sentence were so incomprehensible that, were it not for the well-known accuracy of the law reports in *The Times*, we should imagine that there was some grievous blunder in what we read.

The report continued by criticising the judge's hints that a verdict of guilty of manslaughter would be the safest option, asking, 'Upon what possible theory was the crime held to be manslaughter?'

Expressing widely held views at the time, the newspaper insisted that either Susanna Maggs was insane at the time of the murder, as the defence maintained, or she was guilty of administering a deadly poison to her baby, with intent to kill and after much previous deliberation, in which case the proper verdict could only be one of guilty of wilful murder.

The publication then went on to decry the sentence meted out by Mr Justice Willes. The jury had been quite specific in stating that they considered that there were extenuating circumstances, yet the judge had sentenced the defendant to seven years of penal servitude. Only a few days before Susanna Maggs's trial, a labourer at Lichfield had been charged with the murder of his brother-in-law by stabbing him in the bowels with a knife. When the Grand Jury failed to find a true bill against Martin Cuncannon for the wilful murder of James Frain, the charge against him was reduced to one of manslaughter and he was found guilty as charged. Mr Justice Shee told Cuncannon that, if it wasn't for the fact that he had received good character references, he would be facing a much longer sentence, before ordering him to be imprisoned for just four months.

Mr Justice Willes. (Author's collection)

Above: *The Old Prison, Bristol. (Author's collection)*

Left: *Gatehouse on Cumberland Road – all that remains of the Old Prison. (© N. Sly)*

'What are we to think of the present state of English law, which permits such outrageous inconsistencies, both as to the interpretation of the nature of acts in themselves criminal and in the severity of punishments inflicted?' asked the reporter, indignantly.

Unfortunately, it has proved impossible to discover what happened to Susanna Maggs after her trial.

Note: Although Susanna Maggs is described only as 'irregular and improvident in her habits', there is a hint in the contemporary accounts of the case that she might possibly have been addicted to opium. Although such an addiction is not specifically mentioned, surgeon Mr Siddall was apparently asked at the trial about the effects of 'taking opium for some years'. His answer was that it would weaken the mind but would not produce a tendency to homicide.

8

'IT IS A VERY SAD AFFAIR'

Knowle, 1873

Edward Abbott was known as a steady and industrious man, whose years of hard work as a master mason had left him financially comfortable. He owned a house in Sydenham Street, Knowle that he shared with his wife, Mary Jane, and their five children, along with other properties in the area. By 1873, Abbott was working as the main contractor at Arno's Vale Cemetery, where he and the five men he employed were responsible for all the brickwork and masonry, including the construction of vaults and the erection of tombstones. However, while Abbott might have been a very successful businessman, his personal life was far from happy. He and his wife had lost three children in recent years and their marriage was slowly falling apart.

As the arguments between Edward and Mary grew in frequency and intensity, Edward increasingly sought solace in drink and both he and Mary tried to avoid spending time in each other's company, with Edward often leaving home for a week or two at a time. On one occasion, Mary Abbott contacted the police to report her husband missing and, soon afterwards, received notification that he was in King's College Hospital in London, having been fished out of the River Thames. In trying unsuccessfully to commit suicide, he had sustained a severe head wound when he collided with something in the water.

Mary rushed to London to fetch her husband, arriving to find that he had discharged himself from hospital and that nobody there knew where he had gone. When Edward Abbott finally returned to Bristol, he seemed a changed man, almost as if his mind were elsewhere. He was moody and uncommunicative, shaking his head and smiling vacantly if anybody tried to ask him what was wrong. He suffered from headaches and stomach pains and Mary often bathed his head with vinegar and water or applied cold compresses to his forehead in an effort to ease his pain.

On 7 July 1873, Edward was unexpectedly away from home, returning at eight o'clock on the evening of 8 July with no explanation as to where he had been. Not that there was anyone at home demanding to know his whereabouts, since Mary was out at a concert in Colston Hall when he arrived, having left her four younger children in the care of their eighteen-year-old brother, William. Edward and his son ate supper together, at which time William thought that his father looked pale and ill, but Edward brushed aside his son's concerns for his health and retired to bed at eleven o'clock.

William shared a bedroom with Maria, his three-year-old sister, and in the early hours of the morning, his sleep was disturbed by his mother returning home. Mary went to the master bedroom and immediately a noisy quarrel began between husband and wife. William eventually lost patience with his warring parents and shouted to them to be quiet, at which Mary stormed downstairs, where she presumably slept on a couch.

Colston Hall. (Author's collection)

Sydenham Street, 2010. (© N. Sly)

King's College Hospital, London. (Author's collection)

At four o'clock the next morning, Mary woke William to go to his job at the cemetery, where he worked with his father. William worked until eight o'clock before returning home for his breakfast, finding that his father had arrived before him and had already eaten. While William was tucking into his food, his father appeared in the kitchen in his stockinged feet and began to put on his boots. Telling William not to dawdle over his meal and to hurry back to work, Edward then left the house to return to the cemetery himself.

Having prepared the meal for her husband and son, Mary popped out to speak to one of the neighbours and, while she was outside, seven-year-old Sarah Jane came downstairs demanding her breakfast. Leaving the house to return to work, William told his mother, who immediately went back to attend to her daughter. As she busied herself preparing food, it occurred to Mary that Maria had not yet come downstairs.

Mary knew that Maria was awake, since Edward had already been up to see her when he came home for his breakfast. The little girl was her husband's favourite child and he would often take her into his own bedroom in the mornings to play with her for a while if she was awake when he returned for his break. That morning, he had told Mary that he had bought some sweets for Maria and had taken them up to her, spending a few minutes with the little girl before eating his food and going back to work.

Mary went upstairs to see where Maria was, finding the child's bed empty. Thinking that Maria might have fallen asleep in her husband's room, Mary went to check and, to her horror, she found Maria lying in her husband's bed absolutely drenched with blood.

Above & below: *Arno's Vale Cemetery, 2010. (© R. Sly)*

Knowle. (Author's collection)

In a state of panic, Mary Abbott snatched up her daughter and rushed screaming into the street. Her screams attracted the attention of engineer John Trott junior, who rushed to see if he could help. Seeing the gravely injured child in her mother's arms, Trott sent a neighbour to fetch Dr Carr from nearby Wells Road. At the time, Mary's first thought was that Maria had somehow injured herself playing with her father's knife, but when Trott examined the child more closely, he realised that the little girl's throat had been deliberately cut and that there was no way in which her injury could have resulted from an accident.

Mary Abbott seemed unwilling to believe this. 'Perhaps she fell out of bed,' she suggested. Trott volunteered to go to Arno's Vale Cemetery to find Edward Abbott and bring him home. On the way he contacted the police to inform them of his suspicions that Maria had been murdered. However, when he got to Arno's Vale nobody had seen Abbott and no one knew where he was.

Leaving Arno's Vale, Trott's attention was attracted by a small crowd of people who had gathered outside the Roman Catholic Cemetery just up the road and appeared to be peering excitedly at something within the cemetery walls. When he went to see what was causing the disturbance, he saw a man slumped against a memorial cross, bleeding heavily from a wound in his throat, to which he was holding his handkerchief as if to try and staunch the flow of blood.

Trott immediately began to climb the cemetery wall to go to the man's assistance, much to the distress of the spectators, who warned him that the man might be dangerous and could hurt him. Nevertheless, Trott went to his aid. 'Abbott, what made you do this?' he asked, correctly guessing the injured man's identity, but Edward Abbott was unable to speak, having partially severed his own windpipe. Trott asked him what he had used to cut his throat and Abbott pointed to a tool shed in the cemetery. When Trott went to look, he found a blood-soaked open razor lying on the floor.

Trott went back to Abbott and bound up his throat with his handkerchief. Soon, Sergeant James Chivers and Sergeant Christian Dewey of the Bristol Police arrived and a cart was procured to ferry Abbott to the Bristol General Hospital, where he was received by house surgeon Thomas Elliott. Elliott found that Abbott had a deep cut across his throat and had lost a great deal of blood. He was barely conscious and Elliott believed that his condition was critical and that he was unlikely to survive.

Meanwhile, back at Sydenham Street, neighbours had ushered Mary back into the house, where she sat cradling her daughter and awaiting the arrival of the doctor. 'Oh, my God, this is a judgement upon me,' she said repeatedly, as Maria slowly bled to death in her arms. It took surgeon Alexander Carr almost an hour to arrive at the house, by which time Maria had been dead for nearly half an hour. All Carr could do was to pronounce life extinct and begin a search of the house to try and determine how Maria's throat had been cut. It was only when he examined her father's bedroom and failed to find a knife, razor or any other instrument that might have injured the child that Mary Abbott began to realise that her daughter's death had not been the result of a tragic accident but that she had been cruelly murdered.

Edward Abbott was placed under police guard at the hospital but, because of the seriousness of his condition, he was not formally interviewed for some time. He gradually recovered but seemed to have no recollection of the murder of his daughter, a subject that police and doctors alike avoided discussing with him until he was considered well enough to be discharged. Only then did the police formally charge him with the murder of little Maria. Asked by Thomas Elliott if he understood the charge, Edward Abbott replied, 'Yes. It is a very sad affair.'

'I suppose you did not mean to kill the child but it happened to come your way and you cut its throat,' Elliott suggested and Abbott agreed that this was the case, telling the doctor that he was dreadfully unhappy and that he believed that his wife had taken to drink. He still had only dim memories of the events of 9 July and struggled to grasp that his favourite child was now dead by his hand.

An inquest had already been held into Maria's death at which Mary Jane Abbott told the coroner that she and Edward had argued the night before their daughter's death about the fact that Edward kept leaving the marital home and returning either unable or unwilling to explain where he had been or why he had left. As a consequence of their final argument on 8 July, Mary had refused to sleep in the marital bedroom, something which displeased Edward, who told his wife that it was her place to share his bed.

The couple had continued to 'have words' over breakfast the next morning and although Mary was still angry with her husband, she described the dialogue between them as more of a conversation than an argument. Having taken some sweets upstairs to Maria and given some to the baby who was sitting on a sofa in the breakfast room, Edward ate heartily. He was obviously not happy about Mary's absence from his bed the previous night but his last words to Mary were, 'It's time for alteration', which she took to mean that he intended to mend his ways. What she didn't realise was that while her husband sat eating that morning, he had already cut their daughter's throat and left her alone upstairs bleeding to death.

Mary told the inquest that Maria had always been her father's 'pet'. Edward had been a good, kind father to all of their children but Maria held a special place in his heart and he was always cuddling her and giving her halfpennies and sweets. Maria in turn had been devoted to her father. Mary added that, as far as she knew, her husband was not angry with her or with anyone else. He had made no threats towards her or Maria and had no particular worries, financial or otherwise, although the sale of one of his properties was playing on his mind a little. She related that he had been a little strange and distant since his return from London in February of that year but she had never doubted his sanity and never felt fearful in his presence. Although she was aware that he had been drinking heavily, she believed that he had not drunk to excess since he came back from London.

After hearing from William Abbott, some of the Abbotts' neighbours, Mr Trott and the police officers who had responded to Trott's summons, the coroner's jury recorded a verdict of wilful murder against Edward Abbott, although given the precarious state of his health, it was doubtful that the case would ever come to trial. Yet, against all odds, Abbott made a full recovery and appeared at the Somerset Assizes in August 1873 before Mr Justice Fitzjames Stephens. He was defended by Mr Norris, while the case was prosecuted by Mr Hooper and Mr Bompas.

It emerged that, on the morning of the murder of Maria Abbott, her father had visited the Phoenix Inn at Totterdown and purchased three pennyworth of rum, which he drank at the pub. He had then bought a further six pennyworth of rum and taken it home with him – the empty bottle, covered with spots of blood, was later found in his bedroom.

It was obvious from the questioning of witnesses by the defence counsel that he was intending to offer insanity as the only possible explanation for Abbott's actions in killing his much-loved daughter. Numerous witnesses were called to describe Abbott's 'strange' behaviour, which was apparently a subject of great discussion in the neighbourhood. As his wife, Mary Abbott was not permitted to testify, nor were her statements at the inquest allowed to be admitted as evidence. However, William Abbott testified at length, telling the court that both his father and mother had taken to drinking after the deaths of three of their children and that his father had seemed pale and ill both on the night before the murder and the following morning. Under questioning from Mr Norris, William admitted that his father had tried to commit suicide more than once and that his father's aunt had died a lunatic in Wells asylum.

All the witnesses who testified described Edward as a fond, loving father and all without exception mentioned his strangeness in recent months. Yet none had considered him insane, not even Mr Elliott, in whose care he had been in the hospital after the murder and his attempted suicide.

It was Mr Norris's job to convince the jury that, at the time of the murder of his daughter, Edward Abbott had been of unsound mind. Intending to commit suicide, he had been unwilling to leave behind his favourite child in the care of a woman who he believed was drinking to excess. On cross-examination, Norris teased several concessions from Dr Carr, who eventually agreed that Abbott's repeated attempts at suicide, coupled with his recent changes in behaviour might be considered evidence of insanity. 'At least, I should consider it a case worth watching,' Carr admitted.

In his summary of the case for the jury, the judge advised them to consider two points. Was Edward Abbott labouring under such a disease of the mind at the time of his daughter's death that he did not know the nature and quality of the act he was committing? Or, was he a brooding, melancholy man who had deliberately cut his child's throat after quarrelling with his wife? In the first instance, the appropriate verdict would be an acquittal but, if the jury were of the opinion that the defendant was well aware of what he was doing, then it was quite plainly and simply a case of murder.

The jury deliberated for almost thirty minutes, returning to say that, although it pained them greatly, they could see no other alternative but a verdict of 'Guilty of wilful murder'. However, they recommended mercy for Abbott on account of the earlier deaths of three of his children and what they described as 'domestic trial'.

Edward Abbott accepted the verdict without flinching. Asked by the judge if he had anything to say before sentence was pronounced, he stated:

I shall die innocent as far as I am concerned. I am innocent as far as all my knowledge is concerned and therefore I shall die a martyr to my country. I am committed on exceedingly slender evidence – it is almost like a perjured case. Except my son – I say nothing about him – but two thirds of the evidence is false. Therefore, I say I have been dealt very wrongly with. That is the only consolation I have.

The judge pronounced sentence of death on Edward Abbott, who continued to appear unconcerned, asking only if he might see his wife.

Abbott was eventually reprieved on the grounds of insanity. He was sent to Broadmoor Criminal Lunatic Asylum, where he was still an inmate in 1881. Ten years later, his name no longer appears as a patient, although there is a Zebedee Abbott listed who is the right age and is described as a 'bricklayer's labourer'. If Zebedee and Edward Abbott are one and the same person, Abbott apparently died aged seventy-seven in 1909.

Note: Some accounts of the murder state that Edward and Mary Abbott had six children living at home rather than five, and William Abbott's age is variously given as between fifteen and eighteen years. In 1871, the census shows that there were five children and that William was then fifteen. Another baby was born between 1871 and 1873 and was still alive at the time of the murder, although given that Edward and Mary had lost three children, the exact number cannot be determined.

9

'YOUR CRUELTY WAS WICKED AND DELIBERATE, UNPROVOKED AND UNEXCUSED'

Knowle, 1874

As will be evident on reading the following account, there is some doubt as to precisely where the death of the victim occurred. Since the body was found near Bedminster and the case is referred to in the contemporary newspapers as 'The Knowle Murder', I have included it as a Bristol murder, even though it might actually have occurred in Bath.

On 12 April 1874, a group of young men from Bedminster were walking along Red Lane when they spotted a large package lying in the hedge bottom. Curiosity got the better of them and one, Frederick Thomas, decided to open it. As the rough sacking wrapped around the bundle fell away, the youths recoiled in horror when the contents were revealed to be the naked body of a young child, its legs folded up towards its shoulders.

One of the youths ran for a policeman and PC Joseph Cridge removed the child's body to the Bush Inn at Totterdown, where it was examined by surgeon Mr George Gardiner. The surgeon found that the body was that of a female child. He believed the child's age to be around two years old, although he was unable to be any more precise with his estimate since the little girl was literally no more than skin and bone. There was not a trace of fat on the child, whose muscles had wasted away to almost nothing and, when Gardiner examined her stomach, he found that it had shrunk to a fraction of the normal size he would have expected in a child of that age. There was no food in the stomach or digestive tract and Gardiner came to the conclusion that the little girl had starved to death.

An inquest was opened into the child's death by Robert Briggs, the deputy coroner for North Somerset. After agreeing with the medical evidence that the unidentified child had died from starvation, the inquest jury returned a verdict of wilful murder 'against some person or persons unknown.' At the conclusion of the inquest, the coroner ordered photographs to be taken of the dead child and announced his intention of applying to the authorities for a reward for information leading to the apprehension of the perpetrator(s) of the crime.

In spite of widespread publicity in the contemporary newspapers, nobody came forward to try and claim the reward. Yet in nearby Bath, several people entertained suspicions that the little girl could be the daughter of a woman named Jane Grant. They began to question her about the whereabouts of Beatrice, her little girl, and Jane gave two conflicting accounts, telling some people that the child was with relatives in London and others that it was 'in the country'. Eventually, in May, somebody thought to mention their suspicions to the police in Bath. The photographs of the dead child were shown to Jane Grant's neighbours in Calton Road and the child was positively identified as Beatrice Emily Grant, who was born on 20 May 1872.

Bath police officers Detective Inspector Berry and Detective Charles Weaver went to interview Jane Grant and when they told her that they wished to speak to her about her little girl, Jane immediately replied, 'That is in London, sir.' Berry questioned Jane Grant further and she elaborated on her explanation, telling the officers that her sister, Ann Ponting, had taken Beatrice to London five months ago, where she was now being cared for by Jane's aunt, a Mrs Gregory of 9 Kensington Place. The police checked her statement with Ann Ponting, who denied ever having taken the child anywhere. Ann also told the police that she had no relations named Gregory living in London.

Bath. (Author's collection)

Berry and Weaver returned to Jane Grant and informed her that they were not satisfied with her account of her daughter's current whereabouts and were therefore arresting her on suspicion of wilful murder. Jane said nothing in reply although later, while being held in the police station at Bath, she placed her hand on Detective Weaver's arm and implored him, 'Do try to do what you can for me. I let it live as long as I could until I was nearly starved and the child too.'

'This is a very serious charge. You are charged with murder,' Weaver reminded her, at which Jane sighed heavily, saying, 'I wish my friends did not know anything about it – it will be the death of them.'

Jane Grant was committed by magistrates to stand trial for the wilful murder of her daughter and it was at the Wells Assizes, before Lord Chief Justice Coleridge, that the tragic details of Beatrice Grant's short life were finally revealed.

In 1872, Jane Grant was working as a domestic servant in Bath when she gave birth to an illegitimate child. She was allowed to return to her job, having placed baby Beatrice Emily in the care of her cousin, Emma Gregory. Jane paid Emma five shillings a week to care for her daughter, although she only earned £10 a year from her employment. However, she assured Emma that the child's father was willing to contribute to his daughter's upkeep and Beatrice thrived in Emma's care.

In September or October 1873, Jane rented rooms in a cottage at Calton Street in Bath, representing herself as a married woman to her landlady, Sarah Marchant. At around the same time, Jane removed Beatrice from Emma Gregory's home and placed her with a neighbour, Mrs Ann Scarr. It was agreed that Jane would pay 4d a day, out of which Ann would buy the baby's food.

While Emma Gregory described Jane Grant as a very affectionate mother, Ann Scarr stated in court that Jane had shown little affection for her daughter and that 'little Beattie' had always been reluctant to go to her. Mrs Scarr had Beatrice in her care for three or four days a week until Christmas 1873, when Jane took her daughter, saying that she was going to look after her herself. However, throughout the entire time that Beatrice was living with her mother, the neighbours were concerned about the child's constant crying. It was evident that Jane was going out and leaving the baby unattended for long periods and, according to Emma Hamlin, who rented a wash house directly beneath Jane's rooms, the child cried all day, her cries weak, like a child 'in want.' Eventually, Emma could stand the cries no longer and, with a neighbour, Mrs Eliza Sergeant, managed to peer in through the window of Jane's bedroom. Baby Beatrice was lying in the corner of the room covered by a piece of coarse sacking and appeared dirty and neglected. A formal complaint was made to landlady Mrs Marchant, who immediately went to confront Jane Grant with the allegations made against her.

Mrs Marchant found Beatrice in a shocking condition. The little girl did not have an ounce of fat on her body and was completely bald. Now aged twenty-one months, she was still unable to walk and had burns on her neck and leg. Mrs Marchant accused Jane of starving the baby, to which Jane replied that her daughter had suffered from very bad teething pains and had not wanted to eat. When Mrs Marchant complained about the child's constant crying, Jane told her that the baby would shortly be going to London, where it would not annoy anyone. Mrs Marchant was far from satisfied and, as a compromise, it was agreed that Beatrice would be returned to Mrs Scarr's care immediately until she left for London.

The child who was returned to Mrs Scarr in February 1874 was a very different little girl from the small but healthy child who had left her the previous Christmas. Describing Beatrice as looking like a skinned rabbit, Mrs Scarr told the court that the child was filthy, crawling with vermin, covered with bruises and quite obviously starving. In addition, she had an ulcer on one toe. Mrs Scarr asked Jane why she had not taken Beatrice to the doctor – the child was still unregistered and had not had her routine vaccinations. Jane avoided answering the question and told Mrs Scarr that Beatrice had been ill. Mrs Scarr recognised that most of her problems were caused by lack of nourishment. She gave Beatrice some warm milk and the little girl quickly appeared much brighter and became livelier.

Mrs Scarr had Beatrice day and night for several weeks and, by the time Mrs Marchant saw the little girl again on 30 March, she appeared a perfectly normal, healthy child, although still a little small for her age and unable to walk.

In mid-March, Jane Grant found another job as a domestic servant in a lodging house in Bath. The job paid her four shillings a week, out of which she paid 2s 6d a week for her rooms and 4d a day to Mrs Scarr. Jane's own food was supplied while she was at work but she frequently took food to Mrs Scarr for Beatrice. However, Mrs Scarr stated that the food she received from Jane was usually bread and dripping or bread and treacle and it was hardly suitable fare for a young child.

On the morning of 2 April 1874, Jane Grant called in to see Ann Scarr at half-past six in the morning, the normal time at which she went to work. She asked Mrs Scarr not to put Beatrice to bed that night as she was intending to send her to London the following morning. Mrs Scarr pointed out that the following day was Good Friday and there would only be a limited train service to London. She suggested that it would be better to wait until the next day, when there would be excursion trains, but Jane was adamant that her cousin was going to London on Good Friday and would be taking the baby with her.

At half-past ten that evening, Jane Grant called to collect Beatrice from Mrs Scarr. It was pouring with rain at the time and Mrs Scarr offered to keep Beatrice over-night, saying that she would be up early in the morning and Jane could pick Beatrice up then. Jane insisted that her relatives were leaving for London very early and that they must take the baby. Mrs Scarr reluctantly handed over Beatrice to her mother and watched her carry the child into her rooms. It is believed that this was the last time that Beatrice was ever seen alive by anyone apart from her mother.

On 9 April, Jane Grant asked her employer, Mrs Jane Haines, for a day's leave, explaining that she needed to go home and look after her child. She had already told Mrs Haines that she was a married woman and that her husband was a carpenter, living in Bristol.

Mrs Haines agreed that Jane could have a day's leave from work on 10 April. (In the event, Mrs Haines was about to close the boarding house and terminated

Jane's employment soon afterwards.) On 10 April, Jane told one of her neighbours that she was going to Frome and between two and three o'clock that afternoon she was seen leaving her home, carrying a bundle wrapped in newspaper. She returned home at about nine o'clock that evening and, in response to enquiries from Mrs Scarr about Beatrice over the next few weeks, she assured her that Beatrice was in London and was doing very well, a story she repeated several times to various people until after her arrest on 19 May 1874.

In court, the counsels for the prosecution, Mr Hooper and Mr Stonehouse Vigor, maintained that the parcel that Jane Grant was seen carrying away from her home on 10 April contained Beatrice, although they could not determine whether the child was alive or dead at the time. The baby was found dead only two days later, having obviously been starved to death and her mother could be the only person responsible. Beatrice had been fed by Mrs Scarr shortly before she was collected by her mother and, according to the prosecution, this may well have been the last food she ever received.

Mr Stonehouse Vigor told the court that Jane Grant's rooms had been searched after her arrest and were found to be clean, comfortable and well-furnished. Several items of baby clothing were found, along with plenty of food including meat, butter and dripping. Although Jane had told Detective Weaver that she was almost starving, nobody had ever heard her complain before and her employer, Mrs Haines, had testified that, as well as her wages, Jane received plenty of tips from the residents of the lodging house. Furthermore, Jane was known to use a piece of coarse sacking similar to that in which Beatrice was found wrapped as a window blind and, on her arrest, there had been no trace of the sacking in her room.

In Jane Grant's defence, Mr Bailey challenged the evidence of the identity of the dead child, insisting that nobody could reliably identify the body as that of Beatrice Grant. When she was found, surgeons estimated that Beatrice had been dead for at least twelve days and she had been identified only by means of photographs of her corpse, which would naturally have decomposed significantly in the period since her death. Interestingly, looking at the evidence as reported in the contemporary newspapers, it seems strange that nobody picked up on the fact that since the body was found on 12 April, having been last seen alive by Mrs Scarr on the evening of 2 April, if the child was Beatrice, she could hardly have been dead for 'at least twelve days'. In addition, Beatrice was a small but healthy child, who was fed before leaving Mrs Scarr's care and, since the cause of her death was given as starvation, it implies that she went for several days after 2 April without food.

Mr Bailey continued by saying that several of the people who positively identified Beatrice Grant from the photographs barely knew the child, having seen her no more than once or twice in her life. He also suggested that the fact that her stomach and intestines were empty of food could have been brought about by an illness, which emptied the stomach of its contents. (He conveniently ignored the testimony of surgeon Mr Gardiner, who had already stated that a bout of sickness and diarrhoea could not possibly have been the cause of the child's death.)

Finally, Mr Bailey told the jury that the fact that Jane had not produced her child from London could be seen as evidence of her guilt. However, he stressed that she was under no obligation to do so and that it was down to the prosecution to prove that the dead child was Beatrice, that she died from starvation and that her mother alone had caused her death.

It was left to Lord Chief Justice Coleridge to summarise the evidence for the jury. He told them that if they believed that the child had died as the result of the wilful and deliberate neglect of her mother to provide proper sustenance for her, then they should return a verdict of guilty of wilful murder. If, on the other hand, the jury believed that Beatrice had died through the same neglect but that the prisoner had not intended for the child to die but had simply been grossly and wilfully negligent as to whether it died or not, then they were entitled to reduce the offence to manslaughter. Thus the jury had two questions to consider – first, was the dead child Beatrice Emily Grant and secondly, were the acts that caused her death done with the intention of getting rid of the child? If they could answer yes to both questions, then the appropriate verdict was guilty of wilful murder. If the answer to both of the questions was no, they should acquit the defendant and finally, if they answered yes to the first question and no to the second, the correct verdict would be guilty of manslaughter.

Coleridge became quite emotional as he painted a picture for the jury of a hungry baby left alone to cry its heart out for endless hours on a cold winter's day, in a room with no fire and only a piece of sacking for a blanket. He dealt with the evidence of identity, pointing out that one of the people who had positively identified the child as Beatrice Grant was Mrs Scarr who had cared for the child for some time. He also reminded the jury that the dead child had an ulcer on the toe of its left foot and that several witnesses had stated that Beatrice had a similar wound prior to her disappearance. He quoted Jane Grant's words to Detective Weaver, which he said amounted almost to a confession of her guilt.

The judge then asked why on earth Jane Grant should not produce her daughter in court if the little girl was, as she maintained, alive and well in London. Coleridge said that this could have been done at the court's expense and would have conclusively proved Jane Grant's innocence beyond all doubt.

The jury needed less than thirty minutes of deliberation to return with a verdict of 'guilty of wilful murder' against Jane Grant. Lord Chief Justice Coleridge donned the square of black silk signifying that he was about to impart sentence of death and struggled against tears to address the defendant:

> Your murder was a ruthless one, for you, a mother, killed your child and it was cruel, for you killed it with long-drawn sufferings, which you saw but which you would not spare it – sufferings which it was too weak and feeble to escape from or to resist but which it was not too young to feel. Your cruelty was wicked and deliberate, unprovoked and unexcused.

Coleridge barely managed to pronounce the sentence before he burst into sobs, burying his face in his hands.

Lord Chief Justice Coleridge. (Author's collection)

Twenty-six-year-old Jane Grant had sat impassively throughout her entire trial and, apart from a slight paling of her cheeks, accepted her sentence without any apparent emotion or concern. However, once she had left the court, the realisation of her fate seemed to dawn on her and she began to display symptoms of violent insanity. Incarcerated in Taunton Gaol, a period of complete paralysis followed, and for three days she was completely unable to move, eat or drink, giving her warders grave doubts about whether or not she would survive. She insisted that her recent trial had never happened and, according to the contemporary newspapers, her madness was 'complete'.

Curiously, since no attempt had been made in court to offer insanity as a defence, it now emerged that she had long shown predispositions towards insanity. She had once tried to commit suicide by taking poison and, on one occasion while she was in service, had dressed up in her master's clothes and falsely reported that she had been robbed. Only after her trial and sentence was any examination made of her mental state, at which she was deemed clinically insane. Her death sentence was commuted and she was sent to the Female Convict Prison at Knaphill, near Woking, in Surrey.

10

'IT IS A VERY HARD CASE'

St Augustine's, 1876

The woman who approached tailor John Dwyer in January 1876, asking to rent rooms in his house in Wells Street, assured him that the man who accompanied her was her nephew. On that basis, it was agreed that Mrs Legg would take one room in Dwyer's house and that her nephew, Thomas Allen, would share a second room with Mrs Legg's fifteen-year-old son, William. A young child that Mrs Legg looked after would sleep with Mrs Legg. Within a few weeks of moving into the house, the four tenants were joined by Mrs Legg's twenty-three-year-old daughter, Mary Ann Elizabeth Legg, who also slept in her mother's room.

Thomas Allen worked as a shoemaker. He was known as a respectable, hard-working and temperate man, yet in spite of what Mrs Legg had told their landlord, he was not related to her in any way.

Mrs Legg had been married for twenty-two years to Edward Legg, variously described in the contemporary newspapers as a 'deal runner' and a 'labourer' and, for the past nine years, Thomas Allen had lodged at the Leggs' home in College Crescent. Edward Legg left the marriage shortly after Christmas of 1875, unshakeable in his belief that his wife and the lodger were embroiled in a passionate affair.

Allen, who shared a room with William at College Crescent, had always denied any intimacy with his landlady and Mrs Legg was equally vehement in her denials of any impropriety. However, the Leggs had another lodger, Elizabeth Evans, who seemed to delight in running to Edward Legg at regular intervals with evidence to the contrary.

According to Mrs Evans, for the past four years, once Edward and William had gone to work, Allen would go to Mrs Legg's bedroom partially dressed and spend up to two hours there with the door closed. Hearing this, Edward challenged his wife and Thomas Allen, who continued to deny that there was any relationship between them beyond that of landlady and tenant. As a result of Elizabeth's meddling, Mrs Legg and Thomas Allen confronted her and her husband and a physical fight ensued, during which both Elizabeth and her husband were badly beaten. So severe was the fight that Elizabeth Evans was later to maintain that the ill-treatment he received at the hands of his landlady and fellow lodger was directly responsible for her husband's subsequent death.

True or false – well-meant or simply spiteful – Mrs Evans's allegations brought turmoil to the Legg household. There were frequent arguments between Mr and Mrs Legg and Thomas Allen, during which Mrs Legg inevitably sided with the lodger. Edward Legg was beaten several times by both his lodger and his wife and, as well as constantly fighting to try and save his marriage, Edward was also at loggerheads with his daughter Mary Ann, eventually throwing her out of the house for her immoral behaviour with the landlord of the local pub, the Blackbirds Tavern.

In January 1876, Mrs Legg moved out of the marital home, taking the children and Thomas Allen with her. Nobody told Edward Legg where they had moved to until 24 June of that year, when busybody Elizabeth Evans found out where Mrs Legg was living and passed the address on to her estranged husband. Legg went to John Dwyer's house the very next day, arriving at twenty past nine in the morning.

Dwyer's young son answered the door to his knock and Legg asked the boy if Tom Allen was living there. Confused by the question, the boy went to fetch his father, who called Allen to come downstairs as he had a visitor.

Thomas Allen walked downstairs towards the open front door but as soon as he saw who the visitor was, he turned abruptly on his heel and went back upstairs again without speaking. Edward then asked Dwyer if his wife was living there.

'Are you Mrs Legg's husband?' Dwyer asked him and when Edward replied in the affirmative, Dwyer sent his son upstairs to fetch Mrs Legg, who refused point blank to come down and see her husband.

St Augustine's. (Author's collection)

Next Edward asked to see his son but when William was summoned he too refused to come downstairs. 'It's a hard case,' Edward said ruefully, telling Dwyer that he had lived with his wife for twenty-two years and she wouldn't even come and talk to him.

Mr Dwyer eventually persuaded Edward Legg to leave but only an hour later he was back asking to see his wife and son, a request that was once again refused. 'It is a very hard case,' he repeated.

Dwyer asked Legg to leave without causing a fuss and Legg did so without argument. However, he returned to Wells Street at two o'clock that afternoon with the same request. By now Dwyer was losing patience with him and told him that there was no point in even sending for his wife and son, since they obviously didn't want to see him. 'It's a very hard case,' Edward said yet again.

Edward made no further visits to Wells Street that day but at ten o'clock the following morning he was back with an all too familiar request. Again, Mrs Legg refused to come downstairs to talk to her husband and again Legg shook his head sorrowfully and remarked to Mr Dwyer, 'It's a very hard case.' He continued to tell Dwyer that he and Mrs Legg had lived happily together until Tom Allen came to lodge with them.

'I understood he was a nephew,' said Dwyer.

'No, no relation whatever,' Legg corrected him.

Dwyer assured Edward Legg that he had only let the rooms to Mrs Legg on the understanding that Tom Allen was her nephew. As far as Dwyer was aware, Allen slept with William Legg, while Mrs Legg shared a room with her daughter and her foster child and in all the time they had been renting rooms in his house, Dwyer had not seen even the slightest suggestion of any improper relationship between them. 'That's all very well but he sleeps with her,' Legg argued. Somehow Dwyer managed to persuade Legg to go, but he returned at seven o'clock, again asking for his wife. 'If I could shake hands with her, I could die happy,' he told Mr Dwyer.

Dwyer sent his son upstairs to fetch Mrs Legg but the boy came down almost immediately to say that Mrs Legg wouldn't come.

'Tell her it's her brother George to see her,' suggested Legg but Dwyer was understandably reluctant for his young son to lie to his tenant and shook his head warningly at the boy. Once more, the lad ran upstairs, returning to say that Mrs Legg's door was shut and she wasn't answering his knocks. Dwyer noticed that Legg seemed somewhat agitated and confused and, desperate to get rid of him, suggested that he should go to the authorities about his wife. Edward Legg left without argument, making his usual parting comment, 'It's a hard case.'

Dwyer then had to go out for a while and, when he returned home at about twenty minutes to nine that evening, he saw Edward Legg standing on his front doorstep, looking as though he had just knocked on the door. 'Back so soon?' Dwyer asked him sarcastically, walking past him and using his latch key to open his front door.

The next few seconds seemed to pass in a blur. As John Dwyer opened the door, he was aware of approaching footsteps from within the house. He barely had time to register that Tom Allen was on his way to answer the knock on the door when Edward Legg pushed past him and swung at Allen.

Allen was carrying Mrs Legg's foster child in his arms. He carefully put the child down on the floor before staggering back a couple of steps, shouting 'I'm stabbed!'

Dwyer immediately ran out into the street to see if he could see a policeman. As he did, Edward Legg walked past him and headed along Frogmore Street, going into the Old Fox public house. Dwyer asked a boy to watch the pub to see if he came out again then went off in search of a constable. John Way, a neighbour of Dwyer's, had realised that something was amiss and followed Edward Legg to the pub. He too waited outside and was thus present when John Dwyer returned with PC Giles and PC Sparks.

Way and Dwyer accompanied the policemen into the bar and pointed out Edward Legg to them. PC Sparks approached him and informed him that he was placing him under arrest for stabbing a man. 'I've done nothing but I'll come to the police station quietly because I know you,' responded Legg. PC Giles asked him where his knife was and Legg denied having one. Giles put his hand into Legg's trouser pocket and pulled out a knife. Taking it to the gas light in the pub, Giles commented that there was fresh blood on the blade.

'There is not,' argued Legg, who was escorted to Clifton police station, where he was charged with maliciously wounding Thomas Allen with intent to do grievous bodily harm. 'I have not much to say. This man [Allen] has been living with my wife and I've been several times to the house and asked to see her but she would not see me.'

Back at Wells Street, Thomas Allen had managed to walk out of the house and was heading for the Bristol Royal Infirmary. On his way there, he met PC Wakeley, telling him that he had been stabbed. Noticing that Allen's clothes were saturated with blood, Wakeley thought it prudent to escort him to the hospital.

Ward 6, Bristol Royal Infirmary. (Author's collection)

On his arrival, Allen was seen by house surgeon Mr Henry Macready Chute. Allen told the doctor that he had been stabbed in the abdomen and, when Chute checked, he found a small but deep stab wound in Allen's side. Realising that Allen was in a critical condition, it was decided that he should give a deposition and magistrate Mr W. Fuidge JP was summoned to the hospital with his clerk, Mr F. Holmes Gore. Edward Legg was also brought to the hospital to be present at the deposition but had to be restrained from rushing at Allen and attacking him in his hospital bed.

'Have you been sleeping with my wife?' Legg demanded.

'No,' replied Allen.

'You have,' Legg insisted.

Allen dictated his deposition to Mr Holmes Gore, who wrote down the words as he spoke them. Allen related being stabbed by Edward Legg, saying that Legg had not spoken to him but had just attacked him in the hallway at Wells Street. Allen said that he managed to push Legg over and run away but Legg had followed him and stabbed him again.

'I have never lived with Mrs Legg as her husband,' Allen swore. 'I have never committed adultery with her. I will swear that on my dying bed.'

'You have, you ********. You know you have,' Legg protested.

Allen was then asked if he believed that he was going to die. 'Not yet,' Allen replied, at which Legg remarked, 'You deserved a great deal more than you got.'

Initially, Thomas Allen seemed to be recovering from his injuries but on 3 July, he began to vomit. The violent sickness re-opened his wound and Allen was dead within hours. When Mr Chute conducted a post-mortem examination, he found that Allen had been stabbed in the left-hand side of his abdomen, close to his ribcage. The knife had penetrated Allen's liver, causing the peritonitis that had ultimately killed him. Chute also examined the knife that the police had taken from Edward Legg's pocket. It had a four-inch long blade and the depth of Allen's stab wound was five inches. Chute theorised that the only way that Legg's knife could have produced so deep a wound was if Allen was bending forwards at the time and therefore he was most probably stabbed while he was in the act of stooping to put down the child he was carrying in his arms.

An inquest was opened by Mr H.S. Wasbrough at the Bath Arms in Lower Maudlin Street. The inquest took place immediately after Edward Legg had appeared before magistrates at Central Police Station, now charged with 'having feloniously and with malice aforethought killed and murdered Thomas Allen.' However, due to an oversight, essential witnesses were not summoned to appear, so Legg was remanded in custody pending the outcome of the inquest. Before being removed from the magistrates' court, Legg turned to the magistrate Mr Fuidge.

'There is one favour I should like to ask, that I may shake hands with my son.'

Fuidge gave his permission and William walked towards his father, who grasped him by the hand and kissed him, immediately bursting into tears and burying his face on PC Wakeley's shoulder. Sympathetically, PC Wakeley allowed him to remain in that position for a few minutes to compose himself, before leading him out of the court.

The coroner's jury and the magistrates came to the same conclusion – that Edward Legg should stand trial for the wilful murder of Thomas Allen. Only one witness provided some corroboration of Elizabeth Evans's allegations of an affair between Allen and Mrs Legg. Mrs Elizabeth Hunter knew the Leggs and Thomas Allen well and remembered calling at the Leggs' house some six or seven years ago and surprising Mrs Legg in Allen's bedroom, dressed only in her chemise. According to Mrs Hunter, it was common knowledge in the area that, whenever Edward Legg was away, Mrs Legg and Thomas Allen lived as man and wife. Mrs Hunter had also seen them assaulting Edward Legg, adding that although Legg was the bigger man physically, he was no match for his wife and Allen when they ganged up on him.

Fifty-year-old Edward Legg appeared at the Bristol Summer Assizes before Baron Amphlett. Mr Stonehouse Vigor and Mr J.L. Mathews prosecuted the case, while Legg was defended by Mr Bucknill.

The defence called only one witness, Mr Christopher King, who appeared as a character witness for the defendant. Having known Legg for eight years, King described him as a steady, hard-working and kind-hearted man. The remaining witnesses were called by the prosecution and fell neatly into three camps.

In one camp were the policemen and medical witnesses who described their parts in the aftermath of the murder. These included surgeon Mr Chute and city analyst Mr W.W. Stoddart. Stoddart had been given the knife found in Legg's pocket to examine microscopically and chemically and told the court that he had found blood on it. Although he could not state with absolute certainty that it was not animal blood, the corpuscles were identical in size to those of human blood.

The remaining witnesses could be divided into those who believed that there had been an adulterous relationship between Mrs Legg and Thomas Allen and those who were prepared to swear that there hadn't. The former group consisted only of Mrs Hunter and Mrs Evans, while John Dwyer stated that, although he had been slightly suspicious, he had never witnessed any impropriety between his lodgers and believed that Allen shared a bedroom with William Legg throughout the entire time that they lived in his house.

William Legg agreed that this was the case, as did his sister Mary Ann. Mary Ann told the court that the furniture in the rooms at Wells Street belonged to her father but that he had signed it over to Thomas Allen. She also confirmed that her father had thrown her out of his house because of her 'immoral intercourse' with a man named Harris.

Once all the witnesses had testified, it was the turn of the counsels to address the court. Having called all the witnesses, prosecuting counsel Mr Vigor did little more than summarise their evidence for the jury. It was then left to Mr Bucknill to speak in Legg's defence.

Bucknill opened by saying that he could not dispute the fact that the victim had died from a wound inflicted by his client's hand. However, the prosecution had failed to establish any malice aforethought. Edward Legg was not a violent, passionate or malicious man – he was a long-suffering man who was bereft, deserted and abandoned by all those he loved. Legg had good reason for supposing that his wife and

Thomas Allen were committing adultery and her refusal to see him had provoked his angry passions. Bucknill maintained that immediately prior to the stabbing, Allen had knocked Legg over and slammed the house door in his face, giving rise to further provocation.

The judge then addressed the jury, carefully explaining the differences between murder and manslaughter. Amphlett told the jury that, as far as he could see, there was little evidence of any adulterous intercourse between the victim and Mrs Legg and, even if there had been, there was no excuse for the prisoner to deliberately commit a murder. According to Amphlett, he could see little about the case to merit a reduction of the charge against Legg from murder to manslaughter.

The jury then retired to consider their verdict, leaving Amphlett to try another case in their absence. By a curious twist of fate, the next case on the court's agenda was *Harris v. Legg* and the defendant was none other than Mary Ann Legg. The court heard that Mary Ann had been living with Thomas Harris as man and wife at the time of his death and that Harris had given her some jewellery and clothes, as well as two deposit notes with a combined value of £250. Twenty years earlier, Harris had married another woman and, although they parted soon afterwards, they remained legally married. After Thomas Harris's death, his widow got to hear about the gifts he had made to Mary Ann and decided that, as his legal wife, she should have inherited them. Mrs Harris maintained that her husband was not in full command of his mental faculties when he died and consequently his gifting of money and property to Mary Ann was invalid.

The prosecuting counsel had outlined the case and was just about to call Mrs Harris as his first witness when news reached the court that, after nearly an hour of deliberation, the jury had reached their verdict on the murder case. They returned to pronounce Edward Legg 'Guilty' of the wilful murder of Thomas Allen, although they believed that the amount of provocation that he had received merited their strongest recommendation for mercy.

On hearing this, Edward Legg burst into tears, burying his face in his hands and sobbing loudly as Baron Amphlett promised to forward the jury's recommendation to the proper authorities so that the Queen could deal with it as she saw fit. In the meantime, Amphlett sentenced Legg to be executed, after which his body was to be buried within the confines of the prison walls.

Less than three weeks later, it was announced that Legg had been reprieved and his death sentence commuted to one of life imprisonment. Records seem to indicate that he was sent to HM Convict Prison at Portsmouth and that he died in the Portsmouth area in 1886, presumably while still incarcerated.

Note: When news of Legg's reprieve was broken in the contemporary newspapers, the judge at his trial is named as Mr Justice Blackburn. Since reports of the trial itself cite Baron Amphlett as the presiding judge, I have assumed that they are correct.

11

'WHAT HAVE YOU BEEN AND DONE?'

St James, 1876

Amelia Deacon married her husband, Edward, in September of 1869. There are conflicting accounts of Amelia's life prior to her marriage, with some contemporary newspapers reporting that she led a 'rather irregular life', as a consequence of which she had an illegitimate daughter and others stating that Amelia was a widow and that Ann Hallett was her daughter from her first marriage.

The marriage between Amelia and Edward was far from happy. Although Amelia gave him no cause for such feelings, Edward was apparently very jealous, and he was also rather too fond of drink. After a year of violent arguments Edward moved out of the marital home. With no maintenance forthcoming from her estranged husband, Amelia supported herself and her daughter by working from home as a tailoress, machining trousers for a firm of wholesale clothiers. As soon as Ann was old enough, she too joined her mother at work on the sewing machine.

Almost five years and three months later, Ann received a mysterious message asking her to meet someone outside a beer house. Curiosity compelled her to keep the appointment and, as she waited, Edward Deacon emerged from inside. He told Ann that he was now back in Bristol and wished to reunite with his wife. Ann informed her mother of Edward's request and shortly before Christmas of 1875, Edward moved back into the house in Barton Street.

The Deacons' reunion was not a success. Within three days, Edward and Amelia were quarrelling again, much as they had done during their first year of marriage. Edward was employed by Cridland and Rose, a wholesale shoemaker in Bristol, yet he worked only sporadically and often spent all of his wages on drink. Amelia was not totally without blame for the arguments. She too enjoyed a drink and, after a few glasses of beer, went out of her way to provoke and goad her husband. Edward still accused his wife of being unfaithful to him, while she laughed at him and teased him unbearably.

There were two particularly memorable arguments, the first on Christmas Eve 1875 and the second on 20 February 1876. On both occasions, Edward threatened Amelia with violence, telling her that he would send her to the infirmary, even if he was locked up for it. 'I will hit you with the hatchet,' he told her in February, when the quarrel was so intense that Ann Hallett took the precaution of hiding the small axe with which the Deacons chopped wood for their fire in the bedroom of Matilda Bryant, the Deacons' lodger.

On 21 February, Edward didn't go to work, choosing instead to go out drinking and returning home drunk at about eleven o'clock that night. Ann heard Edward and her mother arguing in their bedroom and, when Edward got up the next morning, he had such a severe hangover that he was unable to face eating breakfast and he and Amelia went back to bed. When Edward got up again, he announced that, since they could not live in peace together, he was leaving Amelia and 'going on the tramp'. He repeated this to Matilda Bryant, then tied up a piece of bread in a handkerchief and went next door to his neighbour, Mary Lockstone, selling her some string for two pence to finance his journey.

Amelia and Ann carried on with their work until Ann took a break to go shopping. She was away for about an hour and during that time Edward came back, at which Amelia and Matilda Bryant left the house and joined other neighbours at the nearby Star Inn. Edward Deacon followed them there and he too spent some time drinking before returning home with Amelia, where they immediately began quarrelling again.

Soon, Ann Hallett returned home, accompanied by a couple of neighbours, Frances Johnstone and Frederick Silvester. 'It's a lucky job you came back, Annie. You have saved your mother's life,' Edward told her, before demanding that the neighbours leave the house. 'It would be a pity to kill her,' said Mrs Johnstone, who was promptly told by Edward to mind her own business. When Mrs Johnstone remonstrated further with him for aiming a kick at Amelia, Edward ordered her out and, when she refused to go, he roughly pushed her onto the floor. Eventually, Ann and the visitors decided that it might be in their best interests to leave after all.

Once he was alone with Amelia, Edward went next door to Mary Lockstone's house. Mrs Lockstone earned her living selling wood and Edward asked if he might borrow her small hatchet as he wanted to chop some wood he had bought from her earlier. Mrs Lockstone lent it to him and, only a couple of minutes afterwards, she heard groans coming from next door and went to investigate.

The house doors were normally kept open but now Mrs Lockstone found them locked. When she knocked on the door, Edward answered. 'What have you been and done?' asked Mrs Lockstone, to which Edward replied, 'Go indoors and see what I have done.'

Mary Lockstone walked into the house, immediately spotting Amelia Deacon lying unconscious on the kitchen floor, her head inside the small cupboard where the household coal was kept. Mary ran to the front door, where she saw Edward Deacon walking purposefully down the street. Her desperate screams of 'Murder!' attracted the attention of several neighbours who rushed to help. One, William Carpenter, picked Amelia Deacon up from the floor and sat her in a chair, noticing as he did that her head was bleeding profusely. Another neighbour, Jane Coghlan, bravely set off after Edward Deacon, with the intention of escorting him to the police station.

When she caught up with him, she accused him of killing his wife. 'I know I've done it,' Edward responded, telling her that he was going to the police station to hand himself in and that he wished she would go away and leave him alone. Mrs Coghlan was not about to risk him escaping and, seizing Deacon's coat, she accompanied him to the Central Police Station, where she told Inspector William May that Deacon had killed his wife and asked him to send some constables to Barton Street.

'Let me speak for myself,' Deacon said in exasperation. Then, turning to Inspector May, he admitted, 'I've killed her.'

May sent PC George Griffin to Barton Street to investigate the allegations and the policeman found Amelia Deacon being supported in her chair by William Carpenter, still bleeding heavily from severe injuries to her head. She was taken to Bristol Infirmary, where house surgeon Mr Henry Macready Chute found that she had five serious head wounds, some of which had damaged her brain.

Amelia Deacon died within an hour and a half of her admittance to hospital without ever regaining consciousness, although according to Chute, she reacted to the pain when her wounds were examined. Chute was later to perform a post-mortem examination on Mrs Deacon, at which he catalogued the injuries to her head. The five wounds ranged in length from one and a quarter to two and a half inches long and Chute believed that they had all been inflicted from behind with an instrument with a sharp cutting edge, such as the bloody hatchet that had been found in the Deacons' kitchen. Four of the five wounds had corresponding skull fractures and brain damage beneath them and Chute attributed Amelia Deacon's death to traumatic brain damage and nervous shock, along with blood loss.

When the news of Amelia Deacon's death was communicated to the police station, Inspector May charged Edward with 'feloniously killing and slaying' his wife. 'That's quite right,' remarked Edward as the charge against him was read out, adding, 'It was all through my wife. It is a bad job but it is done and cannot be undone.' He then told May that he would like to make a statement:

On Monday morning at half-past seven o'clock, my wife began to abuse me before I was out of bed and while I was asleep. I asked her what cause she had for abusing me and she would not give any explanation of it. Then on Tuesday afternoon my step daughter and another woman with my wife aggravated me and kept on abusing me until I didn't know what I was doing of. In the afternoon when all of them had left my wife asked me to cut her up some wood. I went and borrowed a hatchet from the next door neighbour for the purpose of cutting the wood. In the meantime, as I was beginning to cut the wood, my wife came to me with the tea kettle. When she came at me with the tea kettle I was so agitated that I hit her on the head with the hatchet. When I found what I had done I came to the police station and gave myself up and told what I had done. Before that the step daughter said to me and my wife that it was in her power to turn us both out of doors. I have no more to say. It is impossible for my daughter to turn my wife out of heaven, if it was out of home. [sic]

Mr Justice Denman.
(Author's collection)

Edward Deacon was committed for trial at the Spring Assizes where he appeared before Mr Justice Denman. The case was prosecuted by Mr J.F. Norris and Mr Bucknill while, at the request of the judge, Mr Kempe acted in Deacon's defence. Asked how he pleaded, Deacon initially said 'Guilty' but quickly rectified his mistake, stating 'Not Guilty' in a firm, clear voice.

The prosecution opened by outlining the facts of the case, telling the court that Edward Deacon had stated that he was provoked into hitting his wife in self-defence after she attacked him with the tea kettle. Deacon, said the prosecution, insisted that he had borrowed the hatchet to cut wood but there was no sign that any wood had been cut in the house at Barton Street, nor was there any sign of a kettle in the house with which Amelia might have attacked her husband. Mr Norris stated that he could not see any possible motive for Amelia's murder but theorised that his learned colleague, Mr Kempe, would suggest that his client had been provoked into killing his wife by her actions or even by extreme provocation from words.

At this, the judge interrupted Norris's opening speech to correct him on a point of law – mere words were not considered sufficient provocation to justify murder. 'It is not for you to lay down the law,' Mr Justice Denman chastised the counsel for the prosecution. 'I shall lay down the law to the jury but I could not lay that law down to them.'

Perhaps foolishly, Mr Norris tried to argue the point but was interrupted several times by the judge before he could complete his arguments. Eventually, Denman told him somewhat testily:

> Your duty is to state the facts and place the matter – as you were doing down to that moment – fairly before the jury; but it is not your duty to argue in favour of the prisoner in any way. It is very kind hearted of you but, I repeat, it is not your duty.

Norris had tried several times to provide the judge with details of a test case, which he believed supported his argument. Although the judge did not allow him to finish his sentences, Denman did eventually say that Norris would be permitted to give details of that case to Mr Kempe, if he so wished.

'I have sent for it, my Lord, with that purpose,' stated Norris, before calling his first witness, eighteen-year-old Ann Hallett.

Having described the events of 22 February for the court, Ann was asked about the relationship between her mother and stepfather. 'He was a very quarrelsome and abusive man,' Ann stated, adding that Edward Deacon was addicted to drink and, when drunk, used foul language and quarrelled not just with Amelia but also with the neighbours. The fights usually stemmed from Edward Deacon's insistence that Amelia was being unfaithful to him, which Ann insisted were completely unjustified. She admitted that her mother sometimes made matters worse by laughing at Edward and ridiculing him but swore that she had never seen her mother use any violence towards her husband, neither had she ever heard Amelia making any threats of violence towards him.

Lodger Matilda Bryant corroborated Ann's recall of the frequent fights between Edward and Amelia, stating that the couple aggravated one another, particularly when both had been drinking. Although their fights were normally only verbal, Matilda stated that she had in the past seen both husband and wife using their fists on each other.

Mr Norris then called in turn Jane Northouse, the sister of the landlady of the Star Inn, Frances Johnstone and another neighbour, Frederick Silvester. Silvester and Mrs Johnstone had accompanied Ann Hallett back to the house and both testified that, although Amelia and Edward Deacon had been quarrelling, by the time they left them on the afternoon of the murder, Edward and Amelia had seemed on relatively good terms. Mrs Northouse echoed their testimony, saying that Edward and Amelia had both been perfectly sober and had been friendly with each other while they were in the Star.

Mr Justice Denman tried to establish what the witnesses meant by saying that the Deacons were 'friendly'.

'They were not swearing at each other,' Frederick Silvester told him, attempting to clarify his evidence for the judge's benefit.

'How could you call what you have described friendly feeling?' asked the judge.

'Well, there was no bother at all,' said Silvester.

'But it was not an amicable style of language?' asked Denman.

'No,' admitted Mr Silvester.

As the judge struggled to grasp the intricacies of the relationship between the accused and his deceased wife, some of the spectators in the body of the court tittered. Denman rounded on them indignantly. 'Do not laugh,' he barked. 'It is quite disgraceful in a case of murder for people to laugh when one is trying a prisoner.'

After a few more questions, Mr Justice Denman eventually abandoned all pretence of understanding, saying, 'It might be the language of people of that class of life here but it certainly seems to mean something different to what it does in London.' He added that he hoped that the jury would understand it better than he did.

Mary Lockstone then told the court that she had lent her hatchet to Edward Deacon, describing hearing groans coming from her neighbour's house and finding Amelia dreadfully injured when she went to investigate the source of the noise. Jane Coghlan related hearing Mrs Lockstone shouting 'Murder!' and subsequently escorting Edward Deacon to the police station where he had given himself up. Mrs Coghlan told the court that, earlier that day, she had passed the Deacons' house and had heard Amelia saying to Edward, 'Go and may you perish like stones in the street.'

William Carpenter testified to trying to assist Amelia Deacon and was followed into the witness box by PC Griffin and Inspector May, who were called to describe the aftermath of Mrs Deacon's death and her husband's visit to the police station. Magistrate's clerk Mr T.H. Gore then read out Edward Deacon's statement. The final witness for the prosecution was Dr Chute, who used a model of Mrs Deacon's head to illustrate his findings at her post-mortem examination to the court.

Mr Norris then summed up the case for the prosecution, reminding the jury that no kettle had been found in the Deacons' house, making Edward's defence that Amelia attacked him with the kettle seem unlikely. Norris also pointed out that all the doors in the house were normally kept open, saying that the fact that Edward had deliberately closed and locked them before hitting his wife with the hatchet suggested a degree of premeditation, since he had not only prevented her escape but had also minimised the chances that the neighbours might hear anything untoward going on in the house and intervene. Ever the gentleman, Norris closed by hoping that the jury would give the counsel for the defence the same kind and considerate hearing as they had afforded him.

Mr Kempe then addressed the jury in defence of his client. He reminded them that Deacon's life depended on their verdict and advised them to be careful in assigning motives to the prisoner. Edward Deacon, he admitted, was not a man of calm temperament who might be aroused to ungovernable wrath and anger by some great provocation. On the contrary, he was a man of ungovernable temper and quarrelsome disposition, who used no measured words and, if chiding his wife, was likely to use such brutal language as, unhappily, was common among some persons of his class.

Kempe told the jury that he wasn't going to argue the fact that Amelia Deacon had died by her husband's hand. His client had admitted the killing but that was not the charge against him. The charge was that he did, with malice aforethought, kill the woman. Kempe repeated the key words 'malice aforethought'. Where was the evidence of malice aforethought, he asked the jury?

It was left to Mr Justice Denman to try and untangle the legal arguments for the jury. If they believed that Edward Deacon had borrowed the hatchet with the express purpose of killing his wife or even assaulting her, then they should find him guilty of murder. If they believed that he borrowed the hatchet for chopping wood and that a quarrel had arisen with his wife, as a result of which he had hit her with the hatchet, then again the correct verdict was guilty of murder.

There was not the slightest suggestion that mere verbal provocation from a woman could ever justify the use of a weapon such as a hatchet, in spite of what the counsel for the prosecution might have led the jury to believe. Only if there was evidence that the victim had attacked her killer in any way and so caused him to use the hatchet in hot blood or in self-defence might the charge be reduced from murder to manslaughter.

Mr Justice Denman told the jury that he personally had heard nothing that proved any act of violence by Amelia Deacon, adding that, in the eyes of the law, the presumption in any case of violent death was that the offence was murder, unless there was something upon which the jury could reasonably rely to reduce it to manslaughter. It took the jury less than three minutes of deliberation to decide that they found Edward Deacon 'Guilty' of the wilful murder of his wife.

Unusually, Denman did not assume the black cap while pronouncing sentence of death on twenty-eight-year-old Edward Deacon, who showed no reaction to his situation apart from an involuntary twitching of his throat muscles.

A crowd of more than 4,000 people assembled outside Bristol Prison on 24 April 1876 as Edward Deacon was executed by William Marwood. Only about twelve people, including members of the press, were admitted to view the actual execution and they were close enough to the proceedings to report that, although Deacon seemed outwardly composed, he trembled uncontrollably as he approached the gallows and, on seeing the noose for the first time, his hair quite literally stood on end.

Marwood, who seemed exceptionally nervous and fumbling, had allowed for a drop of 6ft 6in. When the trapdoors opened beneath Deacon's feet and he plunged downwards, there were immediate gasps of horror from those near enough to peer into the pit. The pit was only about 7ft deep and Deacon had landed with the tips of his toes on the ground. The knot of the noose had slipped round to the back of his neck and, with a supreme muscular effort Deacon was able to raise himself upwards on his toes against the pressure of the rope.

Frozen to the spot, Marwood looked on in astonishment and horror as Deacon gurgled and struggled for several minutes until the prison governor, Captain Gardner, frustrated by Marwood's inaction, thrust his staff at the rope in an attempt to push it from the perpendicular and so shorten it. Marwood immediately took the

staff from Captain Gardner's hands and continued to push the rope upwards until, after almost three minutes, Deacon's convulsive struggles finally ceased. Marwood was later to explain himself by saying that the rope had been used for several other executions and had probably stretched and, apart from that, Deacon was a light-weight, with a very powerful neck. Although the prison doctor who performed a post-mortem examination on Deacon stated that he had died as a result of the dis-location of his neck, most of the spectators were convinced that he had slowly and painfully strangled to death.

Note: Mary Lockstone is also named Mary Loxton in some contemporary accounts of the murder.

12

'COME UPSTAIRS WITH YOUR DA-DA'

St Paul's, 1878

In February 1878, George Cockin brought his family to Philadelphia Street, St Paul's, taking a furnished room in a lodging house there owned by Mrs Hubbocks. Cockin was a sober, hard-working man, who was employed as a labourer at the Iron Rolling Mills in St Philip's. Unfortunately, these fine qualities were not shared by his wife, who made Cockin's life a misery with her constant drinking and debauched behaviour. Soon, Mrs Cockin was pawning the bed linen and other items from the lodging house in order to get money for alcohol and by September, Mrs Hubbocks was so incensed by the continuing loss of her property that she complained to Mr Cockin about it.

Cockin was mortified. He assured Mrs Hubbocks that he had known nothing of his wife's activities and that he would put a stop to them immediately. Quite how he did so is not recorded but Mrs Cockin left the lodgings on 28 September, leaving the couple's two children behind in her husband's sole care. She was to make just two visits to see her children, five-year-old Emily and three-year-old William. The first was on 30 September and the second on Sunday 13 October.

On 13 October, George Cockin was not at home and had left another lodger, Mrs Mary Fowler, to watch over the children in his absence. When he returned and was informed by Mrs Fowler that his wife had called with some toys for the children, Cockin was distraught. 'If she comes again, tell her I never want to see her any more,' he instructed Mrs Fowler. 'Tell her to go back with the man she's been along with.'

Cockin's main concern was that his wife would take the children away from him. He told Mrs Fowler that he intended to put William into school with Emily as soon as he could, where he believed that they would be safe from their mother. Accordingly, the very next morning, he took the day off work, first speaking to Mrs Hubbocks to ask her if she would be prepared to see the children to school every day. When Mrs Hubbocks agreed, Cockin went shopping for a new frock and boots for his son, so that he would have some decent clothes to wear.

Cockin spent the rest of the day with the children. In the afternoon he took them out, leaving the lodgings at between three and four o'clock. About an hour later, he was seen by Mary Fowler leaving the Black Boy public house on Philadelphia Street, holding the children's hands as he led them home. When they entered the house, little William decided that he didn't want to go upstairs. Cockin gently coerced him to 'Come upstairs with your Da-da' but William was having none of it. Eventually, his sister picked him up and carried him to their room.

Fifteen minutes later, George Cockin came downstairs alone in search of Mrs Fowler. When he found her, he said calmly, 'Mrs Fowler, do go up. I have killed my children.'

Mrs Fowler raced upstairs, finding William lying on the bed in his room and Emily on the landing, their throats cut. She shouted for help and one of the first people to respond was Edward Mayo, who was in the house at the time, delivering a sewing machine to another tenant.

Mayo bumped into George Cockin as he was walking downstairs and noticed that he was bleeding from a minor wound in his own throat. 'Governor, I've been and done it,' Cockin said on seeing Mayo. 'I've cut my children's throats. I couldn't help it. You can give me in charge or do what you like with me.' Mayo took a cursory look at the two children and, by the time he got downstairs again, Cockin was behaving like a madman, tearing his own hair out in handfuls and throwing himself against the walls.

Mayo ran to the Central Police Station and officers were quickly on the scene. By the time they arrived, Cockin had wandered into the street where he flung himself to the ground, sobbing bitterly and beseeching passers-by to 'Take me away and hang me at once.' One woman, Mrs Hassatt, asked him where the children were and, when Cockin indicated his lodging house, she rushed to see if she could help them. Emily seemed on the verge of death but, as Mrs Hassatt went into his room, William held his arms out to her, wanting to be picked up. Mrs Hassatt scooped him up but immediately noticed that this increased the flow of blood pumping from the little boy's throat. She quickly replaced him on the bed and was later to carry him in her arms to the hospital, while Emily was carried by a policeman and another neighbour, Mrs White.

By the time they reached the hospital, both children were weak through loss of blood. House surgeon Dr George Herbert Lilley examined both and determined that, of the two, Emily was the most severely injured and the closest to death. The doctor and his assistants and nurses immediately began artificial respiration on both children, continuing to try and revive them for almost an hour. Sadly, Emily died within ten minutes of her arrival at the hospital, while William lived only for a further twenty minutes.

On the Wednesday after the murder, Dr Lilley conducted a post-mortem examination on both children, establishing that both had died from blood loss after their throats had been cut. Each child had a single wound in excess of four inches in length, having been slashed with the bloodstained knife found in the room after the arrest of George Cockin. Lilley theorised that the wounds had been inflicted using considerable force.

With his post-mortem complete, Dr Lilley released the bodies of Emily and William to their mother. They were taken to a house at Totterdown, where they remained until their funerals on the Sunday after their deaths. Lilley was later to find out that relatives of Mrs Cockin had displayed the children's bodies to the public, charging people a penny each to view them.

An inquest was opened at the hospital by coroner Mr H.S. Wasbrough. After hearing evidence from Dr Lilley and PC Robert Williams, who was one of the first officers to arrive at the house in response to Mr Mayo's urgent summons, the coroner told his jury that there was only one possible verdict. All the evidence pointed to the fact that George Cockin had murdered his two children and therefore they should return a verdict of wilful murder against him. It was not for the jury to speculate on Cockin's mental state at the time of the crime, said Wasbrough, adding that this would undoubtedly be considered when Cockin was tried. Thus the jury formally returned a verdict of two counts of wilful murder as instructed and Cockin was committed for trial on the coroner's warrant.

His trial opened at the Bristol Assizes on 5 November 1878 before Lord Chief Justice Coleridge. Mr J.F. Norris and Mr J.L. Mathews prosecuted the case while, at the request of the judge, Mr Rawlinson conducted Cockin's defence.

Twenty-six-year-old Cockin entered the dock looking extremely agitated. Asked by the judge how he pleaded in respect of the charge of the wilful murder of Emily Cockin, he burst into tears and said, 'Guilty'. The judge asked him if he understood the nature of the charge against him.

'Yes,' replied Cockin.

'You plead guilty to the murder of your child?' the judge asked.

'Not to my knowledge, not to my recollection,' said Cockin, giving the same response when charged with William's murder.

Coleridge ordered a plea of 'Not guilty' to both charges to be entered into the records, after which Mr Norris outlined the facts of the case for the court. Norris stated that, when arrested, Cockin had been very drunk but, apart from that had seemed perfectly sane and rational and had apparently understood what he was doing when he killed his children. Nevertheless, when he arrived at the police station, Cockin was in such a state that he couldn't seem to understand why he was there or that he was being charged with a double murder. He was eventually allowed to sleep off his excesses for several hours before being formally charged, at which point he was still staggering and, according to PC Adam Willie, who arrested him at the scene of the crime, 'seemed stupid with drink.'

Norris then went on to discuss Cockin's mental state at the time of the killings. He told the court that, as a prosecutor, it wasn't his place to anticipate what the defence was likely to be. However, in this case, there was only one real defence, which was that Cockin was insane at the time of the murders. Saying that he was speaking with the full consent of counsel for the defence, Norris stated that there was undoubtedly a degree of insanity in Cockin's family. Several family members had been in lunatic asylums, including his brother, who had died an in-patient in

1869. Cockin himself had tried to commit suicide on at least two occasions, said Norris. The law on insanity was quite straightforward, he continued. A man was assumed to be sane unless it could be clearly proven that, at the time of committing the act, he was labouring under such a defect of reason from disease of the mind so as not to know the nature and quality of the act he was doing or, if he did know it, he didn't understand that what he was doing was wrong.

If the accused was conscious that the act was one that he ought not to do – one that was contrary to the laws of the land – he was punishable. The jury would hear that, immediately after killing his children, Cockin himself suggested that he should be taken away and hanged at once. He had made other similar comments, including one to Mrs Hassatt, to whom he stated that he was going to die for his crimes and that he was willing to do so.

The prosecution then called their first witness, landlady Mrs Hubbocks, who told the court that Cockin had been extremely fond of the children and had always treated them well. He had also been kind to his wife, in spite of her dissolute lifestyle. However, Mrs Hubbocks didn't consider that Cockin was completely 'right in the head', basing her conclusions on the fact that one of his eyes had been removed following an accident with some molten metal at work and the operation had affected his brain.

Mary Fowler then related the incidents of 14 October, saying that Cockin did not appear to be drunk at the time. She too spoke of the kindness with which Cockin treated his wife and children, although she said that Mrs Cockin's sudden departure didn't seem to affect Mr Cockin unduly. Defence counsel Mr Rawlinson immediately pointed out that, at the inquest and magisterial investigation, she had clearly stated that Cockin had been much affected by his wife leaving. The judge intervened and between them, he and Rawlinson tried to get the truth of the matter but neither was able to untangle Mrs Fowler's contradictory statements.

Edward Mayo was next into the witness box. He had seen Cockin come back to the house with the two children and witnessed William's refusal to go upstairs. However, he described the child's reactions as stubbornness or childish playfulness and insisted that the boy had not seemed afraid of his father. Mayo had also seen Cockin earlier that day engaged in a drunken row on the streets of Bristol. He described Cockin as 'acting like a madman' after the murders, telling the court that he had thrown himself at the walls and torn out his own hair in handfuls. Ann Hassatt corroborated Mayo's description of Cockin's behaviour when she met him in the street. She tearfully related going to the children's aid and carrying William to the hospital in her arms, blood pouring from his throat.

Policemen Albert Brimble, Robert Williams and Adam Willie took the witness stand in succession, describing the arrest of George Cockin and his apparent drunkenness on arrival at the police station. Mrs Hubbocks and Mrs Fowler had already testified that Cockin did not seem to be drunk at the time of the murders and, although Mrs Hubbocks admitted that he had obviously been drinking, Mrs Fowler insisted that he was walking properly and did not appear to be intoxicated.

Adam Willie and his colleagues, Sergeant Priddy and Superintendent Abbott, were all adamant that, apart from drunkenness, they observed nothing while Cockin was in their custody to suggest that his mind was in any way affected.

Dr Lilley gave evidence on his treatment of the two children in hospital and his findings at their post-mortem examinations. He was then asked about Cockin's mental state, admitting that, if there were insanity in his family, a man might be similarly affected. The operation to remove Cockin's eye would not have affected his brain unless his brain was 'bad already'. However, excessive drinking would bring out any latent insanity in the blood.

The defence first called Thomas Cockin, George's older brother, who detailed his family's tendency to hereditary insanity. Their brother, William, had died in Powick Lunatic Asylum in Worcestershire, while their cousin, Jacob Tandy, had spent twenty-two years in Brentwood Asylum, where he remained to this day. Tandy's brother had hung himself while the balance of his mind was disturbed and an uncle and aunt 'had to be taken care of'. Thomas said that, since his brother's eye was removed six years ago, drink had always affected him badly. He then added that he hadn't seen his brother for five years and had not kept in contact with him at all during that time.

Two witnesses followed, both of whom were aware of previous suicide attempts made by George Cockin. His former landlord, John Gowie, stated that Cockin had once tried to cut his throat with a razor, while servant Elizabeth Walker had once prevented Cockin from putting his head into a boiler. Both insisted that Cockin was generally sober but, in drink, became despondent and melancholy. His lowness of spirit normally lasted only as long as it took for the effects of alcohol to wear off.

Brentwood Asylum, 1913. (Author's collection)

A group of Bristol children. (Author's collection)

Having heard from all the witnesses, Mr Norris declined the opportunity to sum up the case for the prosecution, leaving the floor clear for Mr Rawlinson to speak in Cockin's defence. Rawlinson began by thanking the prosecution for their great kindness in calling witnesses who should rightly have been witnesses for the defence. He then continued by pointing out that nobody had been able to come up with any possible motive for George Cockin's actions in killing his children.

Without exception, every witness had testified to the fact that Cockin had treated the children with extreme kindness and that he had also treated his wife better than she deserved, she being a curse on him with her drunken, dissolute behaviour. There was no suggestion that Cockin had any sort of ill-feeling towards the children and, while Rawlinson could not deny that the children met their deaths by their father's acts, he could only hope that the jury would find that Cockin was insane at the time these acts were committed. Rawlinson reminded the jury of Cockin's family history of insanity and of the fact that Cockin had been drinking when he killed his children.

In his summary of the case for the jury, the judge told them that there was not the slightest doubt that Cockin had killed his children. However, far from being a hard-hearted, unkind and brutal father, the evidence suggested that, morally, a large amount of guilt lay at the door of another person, who had not been heard in court that day. According to all the witnesses, that person had destroyed the happiness of Cockin's home and, indirectly at least, led to the commission of this terrible and frightful deed.

The judge went on to correct what he called an unintentional misapprehension in Rawlinson's speech, stating that, in the eyes of the law, drunkenness was not considered a valid excuse for the crime of murder. Yet whereas drunkenness was voluntary, lunacy was not something that a man had any moral or intellectual control over. Coleridge carefully explained the legal position relating to insanity, after which the jury withdrew to begin their deliberations.

In fifty minutes, they returned to court to pronounce Cockin 'Not guilty on the ground of insanity.'

Cockin half swooned in the dock before being removed from the court to begin his prescribed detention during Her Majesty's pleasure. He was to spend more than twenty years as a patient at Broadmoor Criminal Lunatic Asylum.

13

'I NEVER DONE IT – SHE DONE IT HER OWN SELF'

Bedminster, 1878

On 26 November 1878, surgeon Walter Edgar Lloyd was called to a house in Mead Street, Bedminster. Shown into a squalid room upstairs in the house, he found a woman in what he was later to describe as a 'shocking condition'.

Tamazin Luxton (also known as Thomasine Lloyd and Thomasine or Ann Hallett) lay on a bed, semi-conscious from the effects of alcohol. Her dirty face was covered with blood from a wound over her right eyebrow and, as far as Mr Lloyd could ascertain, beneath the blood she also had a black eye and severe facial bruising. Her hands and arms were black and blue and she had a broken jaw and a compound fracture of her right leg, just below her knee.

Lloyd ordered her removal to hospital, calling a cab to transport her and accompanying her to the Bristol General Hospital, where he gave her into the care of house surgeon, William Henry Harsant. Once Tamazin's torn clothes were removed, Harsant was surprised at how emaciated she was. He noted bruising almost all over her body, spotting that her wedding ring was flattened on her finger, as though someone had stamped heavily on her hand. In fact, both of Tamazin's arms and hands were bruised and swollen from her shoulders to the very tips of her fingers.

Tamazin had obviously been badly beaten and her common-law husband, Walter Hallett, was arrested and charged with feloniously wounding her. By 7 December, it was evident that Tamazin's condition was deteriorating rapidly and that she was unlikely to survive her injuries. It was decided that a deposition should be taken and accordingly magistrate Mark Whitwill was summoned to her bedside, along with his clerk, Henry Holmes Gore and Walter Hallett.

As soon as the magistrate and his clerk saw Tamazin Luxton, they recognised her as the same woman who had complained in July that her husband had assaulted her. Tamazin, who gave her name to the magistrate as Thomasine Lloyd, vehemently

Bristol General Hospital.
(Author's collection)

denied that Walter had ever ill-treated her, saying that she had never given evidence against him. However, both the magistrate and his clerk knew her as Ann Hallett, whose husband, Walter, had served a two-month prison sentence for assaulting her so severely that her ear was almost ripped from her head.

Now Tamazin gave her deposition but she was so ill that neither Whitwill nor his clerk believed that she knew what she was saying. She was asked several questions, to which she gave rambling and confused answers and, although Gore afterwards read what she had said back to her and she agreed that her deposition was the truth, she was not thought to be in a fit state to sign it.

Tamazin's medical condition continued to deteriorate and, on 15 December, she lapsed into a coma, dying two days later. Harsant performed a post-mortem examination the next day, assisted by Mr Lloyd. The two doctors confirmed that Tamazin had a fractured jaw and leg, both of which were beginning to mend. She had a one-inch long wound on her right shin, where the broken bone had protruded through her skin, as well as a wound on her forehead. She was generally emaciated and, even three weeks after the vicious attack that had put her in hospital, she was still covered with bruises all over her body, particularly on her arms and hands. On removing her scalp, the doctors noted an effusion of blood on the right side of her head, even though there were no external signs of any corresponding injury.

The doctors also found that Tamazin's body showed signs consistent with her having been a heavy drinker in life. Her kidneys were enlarged and fatty and her liver showed preliminary damage from the consumption of alcohol, although it had not yet deteriorated sufficiently to become what the doctors called 'a drunkard's liver'. There was also an excess of fluid in the ventricles of her brain, which the doctors again attributed to her heavy drinking.

Having completed their examination of the dead woman, the doctors concluded that she had died as a result of the injuries inflicted on her. Both doctors believed that the debilitation of Tamazin's organs alone had not been enough to cause her death, although both were of the opinion that her condition would have exacerbated the effect of the severe wounds she had received, which would have affected her more than they would have done had she been a healthy person.

The charge of felonious wounding against Walter Hallett was upgraded to one of wilful murder and he appeared before magistrates shortly after his wife's death. Once the medical witnesses had given their evidence, Sergeant Henry Clark took the stand. Summoned by surgeon Mr Lloyd, Clark had assisted in taking Tamazin to hospital and had afterwards returned to her house to arrest Walter Hallett. Clark began by clearing up the confusion regarding the various names used by the dead woman. Her maiden name was Thomasine Lloyd but, in 1857, she married a man named John Luxton. She and Luxton had parted and, some years later, Tamazin began living as man and wife with Walter Hallett.

Clark told the magistrates that Walter Hallett was drunk when he arrested him and charged him with wounding his wife. 'She's no wife of mine but a woman I picked up in Wales and brought to Bristol,' Hallett told the sergeant, adding that he supposed that Tamazin had sustained her injuries falling over in a drunken state.

Taken to the police station, Hallett made a statement expanding on this theory. Insisting that he was innocent of the charge against him, he told the police that he had been in bed when he had heard Tamazin falling over. Getting up, he helped her into bed. Hallett told the police that there had been no light in the room, so he hadn't been able to see whether Tamazin was injured as a result of her fall. He assured the police that she had made no complaint of any injury at the time and that it wasn't until daylight the next day that he woke to see blood all over her face and a broken bottle lying nearby.

Hallett asked Tamazin how she had hurt herself and said that she told him that she had fallen into the fireplace. He fetched some water and bathed her face, leaving her in bed when he left the house to go to work. However, he was supposedly so worried about her that he returned three-quarters of an hour later to check on her condition.

Now, he found a bottle of beer on her bedside table. 'You have been drinking beer again, haven't you?' he accused her.

'I took a glass,' Tamazin replied defiantly. 'I wanted it. I am bound to have some beer.'

Deciding that Tamazin couldn't be too badly injured if she was able to get up to fetch beer, Hallett stated that he returned to work and left her to fend for herself. When he got home at dinner time, she was still in bed and a doctor was called to treat her.

Hallett told the police that Tamazin was addicted to drink and that, on one occasion, she had even pawned her boots to buy some, arriving home barefoot with her beer. On several occasions she had been sent to prison for pawning items that belonged to the owners of rooms they had rented and she had also pawned all of his clothes except for the ones he was wearing at the moment.

The landlord and landlady of the house in which Hallett and Tamazin lived gave a substantially different account of the events leading up to Tamazin's hospitalisation. Mrs Coggins told the police that, on the night of 20 September, Walter Hallett came into the house roaring drunk and went straight upstairs to his room. Soon afterwards, Mrs Coggins heard a loud thump, as though someone had fallen heavily onto the floor of the room above, which was the one that Walter Hallett and his 'wife' rented from her.

Mrs Coggins went upstairs and tried to get into the room, but the door was locked against her. Eventually, she contented herself with shouting through the closed door, warning her tenants about their behaviour and telling them that she would have no fighting in her home. Ten minutes later, there was so much shouting, banging and crashing coming from the Halletts' room that she went back upstairs again and repeated her warning.

On 24 September, the fighting started again and both Mrs Coggins and her husband tried to speak to their warring tenants, with Mrs Coggins threatening to fetch a constable and have them put out on the street if they didn't stop. The threat of eviction put a temporary halt to the violence but, the very next day, Walter Hallett came home drunk again and the fight started anew.

Mrs Coggins went upstairs, finding Tamazin Luxton standing on the landing outside their room, apparently too afraid to go inside. Mrs Coggins told her to keep the noise down but before long, the banging and thumping noises started again.

Having shouted upstairs several times, Mrs Coggins finally went up to sort her tenants out. This time, she was able to get into the room, where she found Walter Hallett sitting on the edge of the bed undressing. Meanwhile, Tamazin lay insensible on the floor, her clothes torn. There was a large quantity of water surrounding her, as if someone had tipped it over her to try and bring her round.

Mrs Coggins confronted Walter Hallett, who told her that Tamazin had fallen down drunk and that he would put her to bed.

'Do you mean to let her stop there and die?' she asked him, to which Walter replied, 'How can I live with a woman such as this?'

'Better leave her altogether than bide here and kill her,' suggested Mrs Coggins.

Before too long, the all too familiar sounds of fighting resumed and, this time, Thomas Coggins went upstairs to try and bring some much-needed peace to the household.

He found Tamazin still lying senseless on the floor. Walter Hallett stood over her with a leather strap and Coggins saw him strike Tamazin with it. Coggins told Hallett that if he didn't calm down, he would fetch a constable, a threat he repeated when he was forced to go upstairs once again to break up the fight. Now, he saw Walter Hallett kicking his prostrate wife and remonstrated with him for his cruelty to her. Then, for some unknown reason, Mr and Mrs Coggins went to bed, without making good their threat to call the police, leaving their lodger to her fate.

At between one and two o'clock in the morning, they were awakened by a woman's voice shouting, 'Oh God, don't!' and, once again, they did nothing to protect Tamazin but simply banged on the wall before turning over and going back to sleep.

Mr and Mrs Coggins saw Walter leaving for work at about seven o'clock the next morning and, once he had gone, Mrs Coggins went upstairs to check on Tamazin, who was sitting up in bed drinking beer. Mrs Coggins checked on her two or three times that morning, offering to make her cups of tea but told the police that Tamazin had thanked her for her kindness but refused the offer, saying that she would rather have beer.

When Walter returned at dinner time, he was accompanied by another man, Edwin Vicary. It is not known whether or not Walter had actually been to work or not that morning – suffice to say he had met Vicary in the Mead Inn and asked him to accompany him home to check on his wife. Vicary was so concerned by Tamazin's condition that he went straight to Mr and Mrs Coggins and insisted that the police and a doctor were sent for immediately.

Taken before magistrates, Hallett stuck rigidly to the statement he had made to the police. However, once Tamazin died and an inquest was opened by coroner Mr Henry Sidney Wasbrough, Hallett changed his story. He still maintained that he had never harmed Tamazin but now told the inquest that she had fallen over onto the fireplace with a bottle of beer in her pocket, which had smashed and cut her. 'I never done it – she done it her own self,' he insisted, describing how he had tried his best to help Tamazin after her fall.

The inquest jury returned a verdict of wilful murder against Walter Hallett, who was committed for trial on the coroner's warrant, as well as by order of the magistrates. His trial opened at the Bristol Assize Court on 15 February 1879, before Mr Justice Mellor. The case was prosecuted by Mr Stonehouse Vigor and Mr Charles Mathews, while Hallett, who pleaded 'Not Guilty', was defended by Mr Bullen.

Mr Vigor opened the case for the prosecution, describing the events in the week prior to Tamazin's admission to hospital. His first witness was Mrs Coggins, who testified at great length.

The landlady said that, although Tamazin drank occasionally, she had never once seen her drunk, although she had heard Walter Hallett complaining several times about Tamazin's intemperate habits. Tamazin never had sufficient money to buy drink and often begged door-to-door to get enough cash to buy a little coal for the fire. Mr Coggins stated that he had occasionally seen Tamazin drunk, although he admitted that it hadn't happened very often.

Sergeant Clarke testified to the arrest of Walter Hallett, stating that he had found a bloody poker in the room as well as the fragments of a broken beer bottle. Clark told the court that, at the time of his arrest, Hallett had blood on his shirt front and sleeve, although he had explained this by saying that he had suffered a nosebleed and also cut himself shaving.

It was then the turn of the medical witnesses to give their evidence and, in view of Hallett's insistence that Tamazin's injuries resulted from her falling over while drunk, the focus of their testimony was determining which of her injuries – if any – could have been caused by a fall.

Both Mr Lloyd and Mr Harsant agreed that the cause of Tamazin's death was a combination of all her injuries together acting on a constitution enfeebled by drink and that a more healthy person would probably have survived. Both doctors believed that the only one of Tamazin's injuries that could have resulted from a fall was the cut above her eyebrow. The severe bruising and the broken bones were most likely to have been caused by kicks, punches or blows, possibly with the poker found in the Halletts' room by Sergeant Clarke.

The Assize Courts, Bristol, 1917. (Author's collection)

Once the medical evidence had been heard, Walter Hallett's statements were read to the court, after which the prosecution rested. Mr Bullen indicated that he didn't intend to call any witnesses for the defence after which both counsels gave their closing speeches.

For the prosecution, Mr Vigor simply summarised the evidence, telling the jury that he saw nothing about the case that merited a reduction of the charge from murder to manslaughter. Not surprisingly, the counsel for the defence took an entirely different view.

Mr Bullen told the jury that they were not in court to try morals but to establish whether or not the injuries that accelerated the death of the victim were caused by the hand of the prisoner. Bullen stated that no malice against the victim had been evidenced in court and reminded them that nobody in the house had appreciated the seriousness of the situation at the time otherwise the police and a doctor would surely have been called.

The most serious injury to the victim was the compound fracture of her leg, which his client maintained had happened when Tamazin had fallen into the fireplace and hit her leg on the fender. The doctors could not positively state how this injury occurred but what they had been able to state was that Tamazin Luxton was a drunkard, whose body was badly damaged by alcohol and who would not have died were it not for her intemperate habits.

When Mr Justice Mellor summarised the case for the jury, he first commended the counsels for the prosecution and defence on their handling of the case. However, he went on to say that he did not totally agree with Mr Bullen who, he felt, had placed rather too much emphasis on the fact that this was a capital case. Mellor said that he did not want the jury to be frightened or alarmed by thinking that their decision might be the cause of a man's death. Mellor then went on to outline three options for the jury – they could acquit the defendant, find him guilty of manslaughter or find him guilty of wilful murder.

The first was an appropriate verdict if the jury believed that Walter Hallett did not inflict the injuries on Tamazin Luxton. The second verdict might arise in a number of circumstances, for example, if the jury believed that the injuries had not been inflicted with the intention of causing harm or if there had been any reasonable provocation on the part of the victim. However, Mellor stressed that 'mere gestures or drunken epithets' were not judged to be sufficient provocation in the eyes of the law – it had to be something more physical, like a blow or a struggle. At the same time, the prisoner's drunkenness was no excuse for the crime, although Mellor reminded the jury that drunks are generally more susceptible to provocation than most. In order to find the prisoner guilty of wilful murder, the jury must be satisfied that not only did he inflict the injuries but also that he did so without caring whether his victim lived or died and with the intention of causing 'serious mischief.' If the prisoner caused the injuries without such malice then the correct verdict would be one of guilty of manslaughter.

It took the jury just twenty minutes to acquit thirty-seven-year-old Walter Hallett of wilful murder, instead finding him guilty of manslaughter. The judge declared himself satisfied with the result but told the defendant that it was a particularly serious case of manslaughter and that his sentence must reflect this. Mr Justice Mellor then ordered him to be kept in penal servitude for the next twenty years. According to reports of the trial in the contemporary newspapers, Walter Hallett seemed most surprised by the verdict.

Hallett was to serve his sentence at HM Convict Prison in Chatham, Kent and later Aylesbury Prison.

Aylesbury Prison, 1929. (Author's collection)

14

'I'VE DONE WHAT I WANTED TO DO'

St Philip's, 1879

In May 1878, Mrs Charlotte Tilly took a room in the home of Mr and Mrs Way in Parson's Street, St Philips. At the time, Mrs Tilly told the Ways that she was separated from her husband and that her three children would be living with her. However, two weeks after she moved in, Mrs Tilly was joined by her husband, William, and two more children.

There were now seven people sharing one furnished room – Charlotte and William and their children William junior, aged nine, five-year-old Caroline, three-year-old Joseph and twins John and Charlotte junior, who were eighteen months old. Although Mr and Mrs Way felt that they had been somehow duped over the letting of their room, they initially had no real complaints since the Tillys seemed a sober, respectable couple who kept themselves to themselves. Charlotte was particularly hard working and kept the room neat and tidy and the children were quiet, polite and well-mannered.

Yet shortly after William joined his family at the house in Parson's Street, the Ways began to overhear loud quarrels between them. Occasionally there was the sound of a scuffle or a woman's scream and the Ways couldn't help but notice that Charlotte sometimes sported a black eye or other bruises.

As a consequence of the disturbances, Elizabeth Way gave her tenants notice to leave. The Tillys reassured her that they would soon be moving to Australia and asked to stay for a little while longer, agreeing to pay more rent if Mrs Way would relent. Mr Way was bedridden due to a severe heart condition and unable to work, so eventually his wife agreed to give her lodgers one more chance to mend their quarrelling ways and, for a few weeks at least, there were no further arguments.

Throughout his stay in Parson's Street, William Tilly rarely worked. A painter by trade, he was claiming relief from the parish for a medical condition known as painter's colic. Since most house paints of the time were lead-based, those who worked with them on a regular basis frequently experienced the stomach pains and constipation that were symptomatic of lead poisoning. Once Tilly's symptoms had eased, he was encouraged to work to support himself and his family and a job was found for him breaking stone at the local workhouse. However, Tilly found the work too physical, complaining that his hands couldn't stand using the stone hammer and gave up the job before he had even worked a full day.

Tilly was granted temporary relief until 21 March 1879, but when he reapplied, the parish overseer for St Philip's, Mr John Stookes Goodman, noticed an apparent change in him. Goodman visited the Tillys at home and suggested that, as William now appeared fully fit, he should find a job. 'I'm no half-time or half-pay man,' Tilly replied scornfully. Although he couldn't put his finger on the exact problem, Goodman believed that Tilly had either been drinking or was 'not quite right in the head.' Concerned that any money paid to Tilly might be spent on drink, Goodman suggested in Tilly's presence that his relief should be paid in kind. Accordingly, Charlotte Tilly was summoned to appear before the board and was given groceries to the value of four shillings, while her rent of two shillings was paid directly to Mr and Mrs Way. Charlotte was told to come back the following week if William still hadn't found work.

On 25 March, Mrs Way had to go out for a while, leaving her sick husband in the care of her fourteen-year-old daughter, Marina. As Mr Way dozed, Charlotte Tilly came downstairs to fetch a bucket of water, nodding to Marina before returning to her room. Minutes later, there was a bloodcurdling scream from upstairs, followed by the sounds of a scuffle, a terrible coughing sound and then a prolonged drumming on the bedroom floor.

Terrified, Marina ran to wake up her father, who told her to go across the street to the home of PC Henry George Clements and ask him to come at once. Marina ran across the road, but Clements was asleep in bed, prior to working the night shift. Promising Marina that he would come as soon as he had got dressed, he suggested that she went to the police station in the meantime to summon another policeman. Clements dressed as quickly as he could and dashed across the street to the Ways' house. By the time he got there, PC George Pearce had just arrived.

The two policemen ran upstairs and into the Tillys' bedroom, finding Charlotte lying dead on the floor in front of the fireplace, her throat cut. William lay face down on the floor, his throat also cut but, unlike his wife, he was still very much alive, his feet clattering repeatedly on the floor, creating the drumming noise heard downstairs. The four youngest children were sleeping peacefully in their bed, the oldest child having been sent by his father to play outside.

A message was sent to St Philip's police station requesting medical assistance and the children were removed from the room. Tilly then indicated to PC Clements that he wished to make a statement.

'If I hold my throat, I shall be able to speak,' he insisted, going on to tell Clements that his wife had admitted to being unfaithful to him with three other men and had told him that she was pregnant by one of them. Clements wrote down what was said and, although Tilly didn't expand on his statement any further, he implied that he had been provoked into murdering his wife by her admission of adultery.

Four policemen bearing a stretcher arrived at the Ways' house within minutes and carried William Tilly off to the Infirmary. Tilly was most reluctant to be taken anywhere, protesting, 'You are not going to take me away from my children.' However, before long, he was too weak from loss of blood to protest further. 'I've done what I wanted to do,' he said quietly, allowing himself to be taken for treatment.

On his arrival at hospital, he was examined by house surgeon Dr G.H. Lilley, who found that he had a five-inch long cut high on his throat, which had severed his windpipe. Once his wound had been stitched up, Tilly seemed to want to talk but Lilley cautioned him to save what he had to say for the magistrates. Nevertheless, Tilly was keen to ensure that Lilley was aware of the extreme provocation he had suffered from his wife, prior to her death.

Meanwhile, Dr James McBride had certified Charlotte Tilly dead. At a later post-mortem examination, he discovered that her throat had been slashed from ear to ear, severing her windpipe and all the veins and arteries in her throat. So deep was the wound that it had penetrated clear through to her backbone, partially cutting through the bones of her spine. McBride theorised that whoever had cut Charlotte's throat must have spent some time sawing at her neck with a sharp instrument, which could well have been the razor found lying in a pool of blood in the Tillys' room, the blade of which was notched where it had come into contact with the bones in the victim's spine. There were no cuts on Mrs Tilly's hands, suggesting that she had not tried to defend herself against her attacker but had been taken by surprise and most probably attacked from behind while sitting in a chair. McBride was also able to confirm that Charlotte Tilly was pregnant.

With their mother dead and their father in hospital, the Tillys' children were taken to the Barton Regis Union Workhouse at Eastville. Although the three youngest were thankfully unaware of what had happened to their mother, Caroline and William junior felt her loss keenly and Caroline was heard to tell her brother, 'Father cut mother's head off.'

An inquest was opened into Charlotte Tilly's death by city coroner Mr H.S. Wasbrough at the Dolphin Tavern in St Jude's (it was later adjourned and resumed at St Philip's police station). Witnesses came forward to testify that William Tilly was insanely jealous of his wife and had treated her so badly that she had once confided in Elizabeth Way that her life was a burden to her. Charlotte was not allowed to leave home without her husband and, as far as Mrs Way was aware, had only been out once during the ten months she was lodging at the house in Parson's Street.

Whenever William went to work, he would hide Charlotte's clothes to prevent her from going out and he would also carefully position her outdoor shoes so that he could check to see if they had been moved on his return. 'She was more like a prisoner than a wife,' stated Elizabeth Way, who assured the inquest that in all the time that Charlotte had been her tenant, she had never received any male visitors or behaved improperly in any way. Mrs Way also stated that neither Charlotte nor

William had ever been seen to drink alcohol. She was aware that William had spent time in prison for assaulting Charlotte and, although she had never actually seen him hitting his wife, she had heard him threatening her with violence and seen Charlotte with bruises and black eyes, as well as overhearing the screams, arguments and scuffles coming from their room.

The coroner's jury needed little deliberation to return a verdict of wilful murder against William Tilly, who was still hospitalised and receiving treatment for the wound in his throat. Yet while Tilly seemed to be making a satisfactory recovery from his physical injuries, his mental condition seemed to have deteriorated rapidly since his admission to hospital.

He told Dr Lilley that between thirty and forty men used to gather outside his house every morning, watching for him to go to work. These men changed their clothes and their positions on the street to confuse him and, although he had never caught any of them in his house, he was convinced that they visited his wife in his absence, communicating with her telegraphically to ensure that they were not discovered. Tilly insisted that he had seen men going into his house but when he went inside, his wife was sitting quietly by the fire alone and her male visitors had disappeared.

Tilly said he had separated from his wife and, while they were apart, the stairs and passage of his house were thick with mud from the boots of her male companions. He had complained to the police but they had ignored him.

After two days in hospital, Tilly became restless and insisted on trying to climb out of bed. Told that he must rest, Tilly said that he could not stay there any longer and that he would be dead before morning, as there were 'conspiracies and rebellions' going on in the ward to take his life. Tilly told his doctors that his food and water were being poisoned and that some of the patients had attached cords to his bed to pull him out. The doctors were so concerned by his bizarre behaviour that they requested that he should be placed under police guard and a constable was stationed by his bed.

Tilly's delusions persisted until 5 April, when they suddenly ceased as quickly as they had begun. Hence it was not surprising that, when Tilly appeared on the coroner's warrant before Mr Baron Huddleston at the Somerset and Bristol Assizes, his counsel Mr Norris's only defence was that Tilly was insane at the time of the crime.

The prosecution, led by Mr Poole, with Mr J.L. Mathews assisting, outlined the facts of the case, telling the court that there was absolutely no evidence of any kind that Charlotte Tilly had ever been unfaithful to her husband. Then, in anticipation of an insanity defence, the prosecution witnesses were all asked for their observations on Tilly's mental condition.

Elizabeth Way stated that she had rarely spoken to Tilly during his occupancy of the room in her house, although she repeated her testimony from the inquest that he had led his wife a dog's life and that Charlotte had been afraid of him. Tilly had never spoken to her personally about any concerns he might have had about his wife's fidelity, said Mrs Way and she had not noticed any change in him in the weeks leading up to the murder.

Relieving Officer Mr Goodman had noticed a distinct change in Tilly prior to his wife's death. Goodman described Tilly as having 'become stupid', saying that he didn't seem to understand what was being said to him. Goodman had been suspicious that Tilly was drinking, although he had never seen him under the influence of drink, nor seen him in a public house, or smelled alcohol on his breath. Although he had no evidence that Tilly had ever consumed alcohol, Goodman told the court that he had used this as an example to illustrate to the Board of Guardians that Tilly wasn't quite right in the head.

The court heard from Marina Way, then the policemen who had arrested Tilly and conveyed him to hospital and Dr McBride who had conducted the post-mortem on Charlotte Tilly. It was then Dr Lilley's turn to testify.

Lilley described his treatment of William Tilly, going into great detail about his patient's delusions and his persistent allegations of adultery by Charlotte, which he said had provoked him into killing her. Lilley had worked at Warwick County Asylum and thus had experience of lunacy cases. As far as he was concerned, Tilly's delusions were genuine. The judge asked if it were possible that Tilly was pretending to be insane but Lilley was convinced that Tilly was in the early stages of insanity as evidenced by his increased irritability of temper, groundless suspicions and acute jealousy. During his stay in hospital, he had suffered from melancholia and had complained of pain and a sense of pressure in his head and consequently Lilley believed that Tilly was suffering from a condition known as paroxysmal or impulsive mania – in other words, an intermittent insanity. It was Lilley's opinion that William Tilly was insane at the time of the murder, a theory strengthened by the fact that he had tried to commit suicide.

Mr George Gardiner, the surgeon at Bristol Gaol, was in complete disagreement with Dr Lilley. Having had Tilly in his charge, he believed that the defendant was perfectly sane.

The final witness was Superintendent Abbott from St Philip's police station, who was recalled into court to address Dr Lilley's statement that Tilly had told him that he had reported his wife's infidelity to the police. According to Abbott, this had never happened.

Mr Norris called no witnesses for the defence, so it remained only for the two counsels and the judge to make their closing speeches. Mr Poole insisted that up until the time of the murder, there was no indication that Tilly had behaved irrationally, apart from his obsessive jealousy and jealousy alone was no excuse for murder. Rather than acting on impulse, Tilly had shown a degree of premeditation, having deliberately sent his oldest son out to play before killing his wife, even though the child was not normally allowed out after dark. Not only that but almost immediately after killing his wife, Tilly had said to the policeman, 'I've done what I wanted to do.'

Speaking for the defence, Mr Norris described prosecution counsel Mr Poole as 'more of a persecutor than a prosecutor.' Norris realised that the onus was on him to demonstrate that Tilly was insane at the time of the murder rather than on the prosecution to prove that he wasn't, since a man was assumed sane in the eyes of the law unless proven otherwise. Norris insisted that Tilly and his wife had lived happily together until William had been unable to work. Dr Lilley had clearly stated that either failing health or pecuniary or domestic problems might trigger insanity and, on the day of the murder, it was indisputable that William Tilly was suffering from all three factors. Other than her husband's delusions of infidelity, there was no motive for the murder of Charlotte Tilly and it was therefore the contention of the defence that Tilly was insane at the time and so did not appreciate the nature and quality of his act, nor understand that what he was doing was against the laws of God and man.

Mr Baron Huddleston opened his summary of the evidence for the jury by saying he was relieved that it was for them to decide on the question of sanity rather than him. He asked them to consider the evidence carefully, saying that, while the law made allowances for the infirmity of human nature, if every murderer was judged insane then great crimes would remain unpunished. Taken in isolation, delusions were not indicative of insanity, since many men managed to function almost normally while experiencing delusions. On the other hand, insanity did not necessarily mean that a man should be a raving lunatic in a 'strait waistcoat' – it was sufficient that ill health or some other cause had upset his mental balance.

The jury obviously gave the matter their full consideration, since they deliberated for almost three and a half hours before returning their verdict. William Tilly was pronounced 'Guilty' but with a strong recommendation to mercy, since the jury believed that the murder was committed through weakness of mind, even though they felt that Tilly had been aware of what he was doing at the time.

Broadmoor Asylum, 1906. (Author's collection)

Tilly listened without emotion as Mr Baron Huddleston sentenced him to be executed for the wilful murder of his wife. However, soon after the conclusion of the trial, thirty-seven-year-old Tilly was reprieved and sent to Broadmoor Criminal Lunatic Asylum, where he was to remain for many years.

Note: In some contemporary accounts of the murder, the family is alternatively named either Trilly or Trilley. Tilly seems to be the correct name as documented on official records.

15

'HE MAY COME BACK AND HE MAY NOT'

Floating Harbour, 1885

On 21 February 1885, PC Charles Humphries and his colleague PC Phillips of the Bristol Water Police were working in their boat near the stone bridge where the river Froom entered the Floating Harbour. The two constables had rowed under the archway when, a few yards further along the river, they spotted the body of a child floating face down in the water.

The policemen fished the body out of the water and took it to the mortuary at Bedminster police station, where it was examined by police surgeon Mr J. Paul Bush. It was the body of a well-nourished little boy, who Bush estimated was between four and five years old. The child had no marks of violence anywhere on his body and was dressed in decent clothes. Bush believed that the child had drowned and that he had probably been in the river for less than twenty-four hours.

The police had received no reports of any missing children and there were no identifying marks on any of the boy's garments. Hence they published a description of the child in the Bristol newspapers, in the hope that somebody would be able to name him. He was described as having a light complexion, light brown hair and grey eyes and was wearing a 'mixture cloth' jacket, vest and knickerbockers, a white cotton shirt, white socks and elastic-sided boots, slightly worn at the toes. There was also a piece of flannel on the boy's chest.

When Mrs Fanny Vickery read the article in her daily paper, she immediately thought that the child sounded exactly like the little boy she had been caring for since the previous May. Alfred Edward Thomas – usually known as Alfie – was the illegitimate child of Amelia Thomas, a domestic servant who held a position in Redland. Amelia paid Mrs Vickery 3s 6d a week to care for her son but had long hoped to get him placed in Miss McPherson's Children's Home in London, from where unfortunate children were sent to Canada to start a new life.

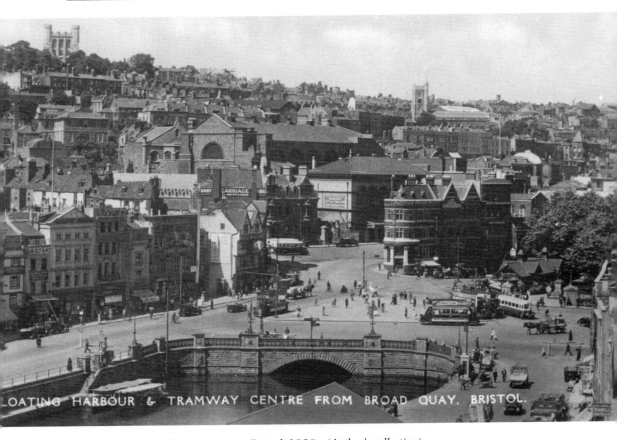

Floating Harbour and tramway centre, Bristol, 1920s. (Author's collection)

On Tuesday 17 February, Amelia sent a message to Fanny Vickery, asking her to get the boy ready for Wednesday evening because somebody was coming to see him. Mrs Vickery did as she was asked but nobody arrived until Friday evening, when Amelia turned up unexpectedly.

'I thought you would be ready, Alfie,' she said to her son. Mrs Vickery was a little put out. 'This is Friday, not Wednesday, Amelia,' she pointed out, adding that she had no clean socks for the boy, having just done her washing. Amelia seemed to be in a hurry, so Mrs Vickery eventually fetched some socks from the washing line and held them in front of the fire to air them. With Amelia rushing her, saying that she had to be back at her place of employment by half-past nine, Mrs Vickery gave the child a quick wash and dressed him to go out.

'He may come back and he may not,' Amelia told her as she hurried off, holding her son's hand. 'I shall not be able to tell you until you see me again.'

Three quarters of an hour later, Amelia was back, asking for Alfie's clothes. Mrs Vickery reminded her that the child's clothes were hanging on the washing line, but Amelia insisted that she would take them, wet or dry. Mrs Vickery began to fold the damp garments but again Amelia was too impatient to wait long. 'That will do. They have clothes for it,' she chivvied Mrs Vickery, adding that she would be back soon.

It was a further forty-five minutes before she returned, this time to collect an umbrella she had left at Mrs Vickery's house. Alfie was not with her and Amelia told Mrs Vickery that he wouldn't be returning.

'I think you have acted a very dirty part by me tonight,' Mrs Vickery admonished her, at which tears welled up in Amelia's eyes. 'Are you going to be down on me as well? Don't you think it is enough to part with Alfie without you speaking to me as you are?' she asked, offering Mrs Vickery a month's money as compensation for having taken her charge away at such short notice.

'I only want what's due to me,' Mrs Vickery protested and Amelia promised that she would return the following Tuesday to pay what she owed. Amelia then went back to her place of work, escorted by James Tyrrell, who was Mrs Vickery's lodger. James had known Amelia for almost two years and had his heart set on marrying her one day.

Now, having read the account of the unidentified boy in the local newspaper, Mrs Vickery strongly suspected that he was Alfie Thomas. However, the newspaper clearly reported that the child was believed to be between four and five years old. Little Alfie was only three – surely it couldn't be him?

Eventually, Mrs Vickery realised that there was only one way to put her mind at rest and went to Bedminster police station to view the child's body. Far from allaying her concerns, her visit confirmed her worst fears. Finally the previously unidentified little boy had a name.

Mrs Vickery explained the circumstances of Alfie's removal from her care and provided the police with the name and address of his mother. The police went straight to Amelia's employer at Alexandra Park, Redland, where they found Amelia asleep in bed. She was woken up and informed that she was to be charged with killing her child. 'It is no more than I expected,' she responded, asking the police if she might be allowed some privacy to get dressed. On her way to the police station, she remarked to her escort Detective Sergeant Heale, 'It is all mother's fault.'

Taken to Bedminster police station and formally charged with Alfie's murder, Amelia asked where her son was. Told that he was in the mortuary at the police station, she asked if she might see him. Superintendent Harris escorted her to the mortuary, where she tearfully viewed the tiny body. When Harris asked her if it was her son, Amelia said that it was, asking the inspector, 'Is he dead?'

Amelia appeared before magistrates charged with wilful murder and was remanded in custody. She was visited by her mother, who, on seeing her daughter, greeted her with the words, 'What have you done?' She then began to scold Amelia so viciously that the custody officer, PC John Wryde, felt obliged to intervene, telling Amelia's mother that her daughter had trouble enough and that she should try and cheer her up rather than rebuke her. At that, Amelia's mother turned to her daughter and snapped, 'Did you do it?'

Amelia tearfully replied, 'Yes and I only wish he would come to life again.'

Amelia Thomas was committed for trial and appeared at the Bristol and Somerset Assizes on 17 April 1885 before Mr Justice Hawkins. Mr Carter and Mr Greenwood prosecuted the case, while Mr C. Mathews and Mr R.W. Clifton were retained for the defence.

From the outset, the trial was beset with difficulties. Before the proceedings even opened properly, defence counsel Mr Mathews protested to the judge in the strongest terms that he had only been supplied with vital evidence on the previous afternoon, even though it had apparently been in the hands of the police for more than a month. The judge agreed with Mathews that the evidence was submitted very late but could not see that this delay made the evidence inadmissible.

With that, the counsel for the prosecution was allowed to begin his opening speech, in which he informed the jury that it would be their job to determine whether Alfie had met his death by a wilful act or by a tragic accident. However, even if Alfie had fallen into the water accidentally, said Carter, had Amelia shouted for help, her screams would have aroused the whole neighbourhood giving rise to the possibility that the child might have been saved. Mr Carter continued to outline the facts of the case but had barely got into his stride when it was noticed that one of the jury members appeared to be asleep.

One of the court officers was asked to wake him, whereupon the jury member, Mark Vincent, told the court that he did not feel well. Police surgeon Mr Bush, who was in court to give his evidence, was asked to examine him. After a few minutes absence from court, Bush reported back to the judge that Mr Vincent was complaining of severe pains in the head and had a very fast pulse. Vincent was epileptic and had suffered a fit earlier that day. Bush told Mr Justice Hawkins that he believed that the juror's symptoms were consistent with another fit approaching and that, in his opinion, Mr Vincent was not medically capable of serving on the jury and giving the case his full attention.

Mr Hawkins decided that the jury must be discharged and a new jury sworn, although the counsels for the prosecution and defence stated that they would be happy for the existing jury to remain if Mr Vincent could be replaced. Eventually, Mr Walter Tarr became the twelfth juror and Mr Carter began his opening speech again.

Carter told the court that although twenty-two-year-old Amelia had always been a loving mother to little Alfie, she received no financial support from the boy's father to help with his care. For the first two years of his life, Alfie had been placed with a woman named Mrs Watkins but Amelia had then employed Mrs Vickery to care for him, paying her 3s 6d a week for doing so. The total cost of keeping Alfie with Mrs Vickery was more than £9 a year and Amelia's annual wage was only £11. She had therefore hoped to place the boy in a home but those hopes had been dashed in a letter found in her room after her arrest. The letter, from Amelia's sister-in-law, Mrs Evangeline Thomas, informed her that a woman had called to say that there was no possibility that Alfie could be admitted to the home due to his illegitimacy. Had Amelia been a widow, things might have been different but it was the policy of Miss McPherson's home that illegitimate children were not accepted.

The prosecution then called their first witness, PC Humphries, who had retrieved Alfie's body from the water. Unfortunately, the prosecution had failed to provide a plan of the area for the jury and were chastised by the judge for what he called 'this scandalous omission'. Had such a plan been provided, the jury would have been able to appreciate that much of the area was unfenced and therefore a child could easily have fallen into the water accidentally.

Mr Justice Hawkins. (Author's collection)

Humphries was followed into the witness box by Mrs Vickery, who related her last sighting of the child alive, leaving her home with his mother. Mrs Vickery told the court that Amelia Thomas had always seemed a dotingly fond mother. She had always been prompt with her payments for her son's care and had visited him every Sunday and at other times, as often as the demands of her job would allow.

James Tyrrell then took the stand, telling the court that he had walked Amelia Thomas back to her employer's home on the evening of Friday 20 February and that Amelia had been very tearful about parting from Alfie, saying that she would never have done so if it had not been for her mother. James had been walking out with Amelia for some time and knew that she hoped to get her son into a children's home. He had assumed that this was where Alfie had been taken. He told the court that he had thought seriously about marrying Amelia Thomas and that Alfie would have been no obstacle to his plans. He added that he had never heard Amelia complain that the boy was a burden to her and that she had always seemed very fond of her son and very loving towards him.

Evangeline Thomas related writing to her sister-in-law on 9 February to tell her that Alfie had been denied a place in Miss McPherson's home, after which Detective Sergeant Heale and PC Rapps testified to Amelia's arrest at her employer's home. There was some dispute about the words Amelia spoke at the time. Both policemen recalled her saying 'It is no more than I expected' but neither could remember precisely when she said them. Defence counsel Mr Mathews argued that this was an important point. If Amelia had said 'It is no more than I expected' immediately after being informed that she was being arrested for her son's murder, there was an implication that she had killed the child and had been almost waiting to be caught. Yet both policemen also remembered Amelia asking, 'Can I dress alone?' The words 'It is no more than I expected' took on an entirely different meaning, if spoken after the refusal of her request to dress in private.

Superintendent Harris recalled Amelia's mother's visit to her daughter and Amelia's admission to her mother that she had 'done it'. At this point, Amelia Thomas fainted and the trial was temporarily suspended while she was removed from the court for medical treatment.

When it resumed, Harris concluded his evidence and, after hearing from PC Wryde and surgeon Mr Bush, who had performed a post-mortem examination on Alfie and determined that he had died by drowning, the prosecution rested.

Mr Mathews, for the defence, seemed determined to portray Amelia Thomas as a tragic victim of her circumstances. Here was a woman, he told the court, who had been a mother since the age of nineteen and had unstintingly and uncomplainingly given almost everything she earned to support her child. Over the past three years, her devotion to her child had not been broken by so much as a single word, deed or thought, even though Amelia herself had been persecuted by someone that she could reasonably have expected to love and support her – her own mother. There was much that was good in Amelia Thomas, said Mathews, so much so that she had won the love of an honest man, who was prepared to marry her in spite of the stain on her character.

Reminding the jury that they held the life of the accused in their hands, he asked them to consider how an apparently tender and devoted mother could, in the space of a few minutes, turn into a criminal with a character so foreign that is was unrecognisable.

Mathews accused the prosecution of 'hazy indistinctness'. He told the jury that there had been no attempt to explain where the child went into the water, other than to say that it might have been at the stone bridge or at the archway. The prosecution had not even provided a plan of the area, nor had they made any attempt to determine how Amelia Thomas had spent the time between her three visits to Mrs Vickery on the night of the murder.

A section of the water near Traitor's Bridge was completely unprotected and it took no great leap of the imagination to suppose that little Alfie might have accidentally strayed into the water and been carried away by the fast currents before his mother had the chance to try and save him. If this were the case then the jury had no option but to acquit his client.

If, on the other hand, the child had fallen into the water accidentally and his mother had made no attempt to save him then a verdict of manslaughter was justified. However, the jury should consider another scenario.

Suppose Amelia Thomas had met with somebody – maybe the child's father – and had persuaded that person to take the child. It was not disputed that she had returned to Mrs Vickery's house, an act that was far more consistent with someone else taking the boy and asking for his clothes.

The judge asked Mr Mathews if he could specifically point to any evidence that showed gross negligence on the defendant's part and Mathews began to repeat what he had said about a section of the water being unfenced. Mr Justice Hawkins interrupted him, saying that while he agreed that Amelia Thomas could have been negligent in allowing her son to fall in the water and not rescuing or even attempting to save him, there was no evidence to suggest that this was what had happened. Eventually, Mathews was forced to concede that there was no such evidence, although he reiterated the fact that nobody knew exactly how Amelia had spent her time after leaving Mrs Vickery's house.

Thus, when the judge began his summary for the jury, he informed them that unless they could find direct testimony to support Mr Mathews' contention that Alfie's death had resulted from gross negligence, or could find any grounds for a reduction of the charge to manslaughter, they should be considering only whether or not they believed that Alfie's death came as the result of a wilful act by his mother. Mr Justice Hawkins took care to remind the jury that they must work with the evidence that had been presented to them in court and that, if that evidence didn't completely satisfy them, they were bound to return a verdict of 'not guilty'.

It took the jury almost an hour to return with a verdict of 'Guilty of wilful murder' against Amelia Thomas, although they recommended mercy in view of her youth and previous good character.

Mr Justice Hawkins promised that he would 'cheerfully forward their recommendation to the quarter where it could receive proper attention', before placing the square of black silk on his head, prior to imparting the death sentence. Before her fainting fit, Amelia Thomas had seemed relatively composed but, having returned to court after being revived she appeared dazed, looking unwell and haggard. Now she seemed barely able to comprehend the seriousness of her fate as she listened to the judge sentencing her to be executed.

In the event, the jury's recommendation was heeded as, only a short while after the conclusion of her trial, Amelia Thomas was reprieved. Her ultimate fate is not recorded, although it is likely that she was transported and ended her days on foreign soil.

Note: PC Charles Humphries is alternatively named Humphreys in some contemporary accounts of the case. The river Froom is now known as the Frome, Froom being the historical spelling, which was correct at the time of the murder. Mrs Evangeline Thomas is sometimes referred to as Angelina Thomas. The children's home where Amelia hoped to place Alfie is named both as Miss Macpherson's and Miss McPherson's Home.

16

'I BEGGED HARD, LIKE A CHILD BEGGING BREAD'

Kingswood, 1892

Several people heard the strange noise in Soundwell Road, Kingswood at around four o'clock on the afternoon of 28 September 1892. Shoemakers George Patfield and Edward Millett, who rented a workshop behind the houses in the main thoroughfare, dismissed the sound as children throwing stones at their door, while to Walter Rowe, who happened to be walking down the road at the time, it sounded exactly like the crack of a whip or perhaps somebody hitting a shop counter with a piece of leather.

Rowe had his dog with him and thought that the noise had come from a nearby shop and had been intended to frighten the animal. He retraced his steps until he was able to see inside the nearest shop, which was run by Jane Elizabeth Flew. A man stood by the glass door leading from the shop into the living quarters and Rowe noticed that one of the muslin curtains screening the door appeared to be on fire. As Rowe watched, the door opened and a woman staggered out of the living quarters, pushing past the man into the shop, obviously heading for the street. However, before she could reach it, she suddenly dropped to the floor, at which the man turned and went in the opposite direction, into the rooms behind the shop. Rowe instantly realised that the woman had been attacked and rushed off to fetch a policeman.

Meanwhile, in the shop on the other side of the road, Mrs Peacock hadn't heard any sound at all. However, as she was serving a customer, she happened to look up and saw her opposite neighbour sprawled on the ground in the doorway of her own shop, in a spreading pool of blood. Mrs Peacock rushed across the road, taking with her Ebenezer Brown, a baker she employed. Together they tried to lift the injured woman but were unable to do so. Brown went to fetch George Patfield, who helped them carry Jane Flew into the kitchen at the rear of her shop, where they placed her in a chair.

Jane was still alive and groaning quietly but once in the kitchen she murmured, 'Oh, oh,' and then died. Within minutes, Walter Rowe arrived back at the shop with two police officers, PC Askell and PC Kent, who were quickly followed by Inspector Ricketts and Sergeant Shaw. Shaw had recently spoken with Jane Flew, whose brother, George Peach, had complained to him about the threatening behaviour of her estranged common-law husband. It was not the first time that the police had been called to mediate between Jane Flew and Albert Manning. Almost ten weeks earlier, Inspector Watkins was called to the shop, where Jane complained that Albert was threatening her life and that she wanted him to leave.

'She doesn't want me now she has her black lamb,' Manning explained to the inspector, who suggested to Jane that it was perhaps unfair of her to turn Manning out of the house at that time of night.

'The man is not right. I am afraid to stop with him,' Jane insisted, telling Watkins that Manning was only a lodger. Watkins eventually left Jane and Albert still discussing their relationship, listening outside the house for some time and satisfying himself that the worst of their argument had blown over. When he saw Jane and the children leaving the house, he felt it safe to leave, although he was called back the next day by George Peach, who complained that Manning had cut some of Jane's clothes.

Jane Elizabeth Flew married her husband, Job, in 1871. In 1874, the couple took in a seventeen-year-old lodger named Albert Manning. Manning and Jane Flew soon began an affair and, although Manning later married a woman named Mary Fry, he left her after just six weeks and returned to Jane. Eventually Manning and Jane left their respective spouses and set up home together, along with the four children from Jane's marriage.

Jane and Albert apparently lived happily together for about ten years and eventually settled in Soundwell Road, Kingswood, where Jane ran a small greengrocer's shop, while Albert continued with his work as a mason.

Jane and Albert had recently separated, with Manning moving back into his mother's home at Warmley Hill. The cause of their separation was another man, although it is not clear if his alleged affair with Jane actually happened or whether it was merely a figment of Albert's fevered imagination. Either way, Albert became uncontrollably jealous of the man he saw as his rival for Jane's affections and she either tired of his constant unfounded accusations or just wanted him out of the way so that she could pursue her new relationship.

Thus Albert moved out of their shared home, although he continued to visit Jane at regular intervals, either pleading with her to give their relationship another chance or threatening her with violence if she didn't. On one occasion, he threatened to shoot her and Jane was so perturbed that she called the police. Albert was subsequently spoken to by Sergeant Shaw, who advised him to keep away from his former 'paramour'.

'I wouldn't hurt a hair of her head,' Albert reassured the police officer and, for a while, it looked as if he had taken notice of the advice he had been given, since his visits to Jane's shop ceased. Now, only one week after Jane Flew had complained to Sergeant Shaw about Albert Manning, she was dead.

Shaw and Inspector Ricketts immediately set off to Warmley Hill in search of Manning. Meanwhile, the two constables and Walter Rowe began a search of the premises and, when they reached the back bedroom, they found Manning concealed behind a perambulator, a large wooden board and some bedclothes. He fought desperately against being captured and it was with difficulty that Rowe and the two officers managed to restrain him until Ricketts and Shaw arrived back at the shop. A cab was called to transport him to the police station and Inspector Ricketts informed Manning that he was being charged with the murder of Jane Flew. Manning took this news relatively calmly but when he had to walk past Jane's body to get to the cab he became violent again. 'Oh, my God, let me kiss her before I am taken away,' he begged the officers, who were more concerned with trying to subdue him so that he could be taken into custody.

Manning was searched on his arrival at Lawford's Gate police station. Although he showed no signs of drunkenness, a bottle of beer was found in his pocket, along with seven cartridges (single 'packages', containing bullet, gunpowder and primer). A search of the shop on Soundwell Road had already turned up a British Bulldog revolver, hidden behind the register grate of the room where Manning was hiding. It contained two cartridges identical to those found in Manning's pocket and three spent cartridges.

In spite of being cautioned at the police station, Manning seemed unusually talkative. 'It's all up with me,' he told Superintendent Boyd, asking him, 'What do you think is the worst they will do to me? Will I get a few years transportation?' When Boyd informed him that his crime was a capital offence, Manning recoiled in horror. 'Oh, my God, don't say that,' he pleaded, before deciding that he wished to make a statement.

'It is all through George Bryant that this occurred through my dear soul and me,' he said, naming the man who he suspected as his rival for Jane's affections. He told the police that he had caught Jane and Bryant together several times either in the stable at the back of the shop or in the living quarters with the door closed and had warned Bryant that if it didn't stop, there would be a row. According to Manning, Bryant laughed in his face and made fun of him.

He next discovered that Jane had been for a ride with Bryant in the shop cart and, when he challenged her about this, she insisted that she would allow anyone she wanted to ride with her. Weeks later, Manning said that he had taken the pony to the blacksmith's, passing his rival on the way and, when he got home with the pony, Bryant was once again in his kitchen with Jane. There had been an argument and Bryant left hurriedly but had then sent a solicitor's letter to Manning demanding an apology.

Manning alleged that Bryant had tried to turn Jane's adult daughters against him and had so poisoned Jane's mind that she had turned him out of their home. He related calling in to the shop to buy a bottle of soda water and told the police that Jane had immediately summoned Sergeant Shaw and asked him to remove Manning from the shop, saying that she didn't want him on the premises. He added that he believed he was a laughing stock in the area after the police caution and that Jane, her daughters, Bryant and some of the neighbours were talking about him behind his back.

A non-firing replica of a Webley 'British Bulldog' revolver. (Photograph taken by Commander Zulu, July 2006)

'I begged hard, like a child begging bread,' Manning's statement continued, as he told the police that he had offered Jane all his money to make up with him. Realising the futility of his efforts, Manning stated that he had purchased the revolver about six weeks earlier, intending to use it to put an end to his love rival.

Describing the day of the murder, Manning told the police that he had left his place of work and walked the 200 yards to Jane's shop with the intention of trying to talk her into taking him back. Jane would not listen and had ordered him to leave, threatening to have him 'taken up' if he didn't. Manning said that he had tried to go into the kitchen at the back of the shop but that Jane had run at him to prevent him from doing so, shouting 'Murder!' at the top of her voice. 'I fired through the window,' said Manning.

Having signed his statement with his cross, Manning appeared dazed and confused, so much so that the police feared that he may have taken poison and summoned a doctor to examine him. His apparent confusion continued throughout his appearances at the magistrates' court, where more and more information about him was gradually revealed as a result of the police enquiries into the murder.

Almost without exception, everyone that the police interviewed in connection with the death of Jane Flew described Manning as a quiet, obliging, civil and inoffensive man who, in the words of his employer, builder Mr H.W. Bullock, was '... certainly not the sort of man one would expect to take a fellow creature's life.' The end of Manning's cohabitation with Jane seemed to have precipitated his complete change of character and he had publicly threatened violence both towards Jane and George Bryant.

The loving relationship between Jane Flew and Manning appeared to have been gradually deteriorating for almost two years. Jane's daughters, Mary Ann and Kate, told the magistrates that Manning had been uncontrollably jealous and that his emotions were especially aroused when he had a drink. Both young women stated that Manning had mentioned other men but that, in recent weeks, the focus of his jealous rage had been George Bryant. Kate, who was in service and did not live at home, had particularly noticed a change in Manning's behaviour and appearance over the past two months, while Mary Ann had witnessed the drunken rows and arguments at close quarters. 'We couldn't stand him,' she told magistrates. Jane's brother corroborated his nieces' statements, telling the court that his sister had complained to him several times about Manning's irrational jealousy.

It emerged that, on the day of the murder, the illiterate Manning had obtained a piece of paper and had approached several of his work colleagues, asking them to write out his will for him. Other than that, none of his workmates had noticed any significant change in his behaviour that day and none had entertained even the slightest suspicion that he was intending to commit murder.

Albert Manning was eventually committed to stand trial at the next Gloucestershire Assizes for the wilful murder of Jane Elizabeth Flew and the proceedings opened in November 1892 before Mr Justice Day. By then, there were grave doubts about Manning's fitness to plead. There had been conflicting reports on his sanity from numerous doctors and it was eventually decided to postpone his trial until the next assizes, to allow him to be observed further.

By February 1893, when Manning appeared before Mr Justice Grantham, the doubts had not been satisfactorily resolved. Asked how he pleaded to the charge against him, Manning remained silent and his defence counsel, Mr Gwynne James, proposed that he was simply not capable of pleading.

The court then heard from a succession of witnesses, each with a differing view on the defendant's mental state. William Wheeler and William Skinner, two warders from Gloucester Prison who had been in charge of Manning since his arrival there on 3 October 1892, were of the opinion that Manning was 'putting it on'. They related seemingly normal conversations he had conducted with his visitors, citing in particular a discussion with his mother, during which Manning squarely placed the blame for his predicament on George Bryant, saying that if it were not for Bryant, he would still have been happy and comfortable with his 'dear Jane'. Manning had also told the warders that 'dear Jane' had visited him in his cell and taken tea with him. However, shortly before the assizes in November of the previous year, he had simply stopped speaking, breaking his silence only once to ask for more food.

Although Manning had appeared dazed from the moment of his arrival at Gloucester Prison, nobody was prepared to state that his mind was weak. He was a model prisoner who caused no trouble to anyone and appeared to understand everything that was said to him. Yet almost everyone agreed that Manning's behaviour became stranger whenever he felt that he was being watched.

Dr Frederick H. Craddock, the medical superintendent of the County Asylum, had been observing Manning throughout his time in Gloucester Prison. He told the court that, until very recently, he was of the opinion that the prisoner was unfit to plead. However, having observed Manning a couple of days earlier through a hole in the wall of his cell and then examined him, together with prison doctor Dr Oscar Clark, he had noticed a marked alteration in Manning's demeanour and had consequently changed his opinion. Clark, on the other hand, disagreed – it was his belief that Manning had been in a constant 'condition of torpor' since his arrival at the prison and that, although he too had recognised a temporary improvement during the examination with Craddock, he still found Manning unfit to plead.

Prisoner Edwin Jones, who had shared a cell with Manning up until the last assizes, told the court that Manning had seemed perfectly rational and capable of conducting a normal conversation, frequently asking Jones to read to him from the Bible. Manning had never mentioned 'dear Jane' to his cell mate, although Jones stated that Manning's behaviour changed considerably whenever he suspected he was being observed.

In summing up the conflicting evidence for the jury, Mr Justice Grantham told them that they must decide 'Is he shamming?' The jury asked just one question – had Manning ever been observed while he was asleep?

Warder Skinner was recalled to answer the question, informing the jury that Manning generally slept soundly, snored heavily and did not twitch. Having heard that, the jury concluded that Manning was fit to stand trial.

Bristol and County Asylum, 1906. (Author's collection)

Once again, Manning remained mute when asked to plead, in spite of prompting by the clerk of the court and the two prison warders who flanked him in the dock. Mr Justice Grantham eventually asked that a plea of 'Not Guilty' be recorded and the trial proper commenced.

Prosecution counsel Mr Acland outlined the facts of the case, theorising that Manning had left work on the day of the murder carrying his revolver, in the hope of catching George Bryant in a clandestine assignation with Jane Flew. Had that happened, the outcome of the encounter might have been entirely different, stated Acland, concluding his opening speech by informing the jury that the crux of the case would be whether or not Manning was responsible for his actions at the time of the murder.

The court heard from the doctor who had conducted the post-mortem examination on Jane Flew who stated that she had been shot once in her left breast, the bullet passing through her body, exiting her back. From then, the purpose of the majority of the witnesses called seemed to be the provision of evidence regarding Manning's mental condition.

Mary Jane Manning, who was married to Albert's brother, George, told the court that Albert had been 'peculiar' throughout the entire time she had known him. George was also peculiar, said Mary Jane, particularly when the moon was full. On one occasion, he had shot a calf without reason and on another he had dashed his favourite dog against a wall, knocking its brains out. Mary Jane told the court that her husband was often violent towards her and that she used to hide the house knives from him and frequently sought refuge with friends and neighbours when he attacked her.

Albert Manning's mother, Sarah Anne Palmer, stated that Albert had long complained of severe pains in his head and that his behaviour had recently become even more peculiar than usual. He suffered from what she called 'attacks', telling the court that, when Albert felt an 'attack' coming on, he would insist that she left the house so that he didn't harm her. In the past, she had hidden knives and razors from him, fearing both for her own and her son's safety.

Albert's father had been equally peculiar, said Mrs Palmer and, on one occasion, had smashed all the furniture in the house without reason. Albert's aunt was described as 'very peculiar' and had once made a somewhat half-hearted attempt to hang herself.

A witness, Mary Johnstone, told the court that Jane Flew had referred to Albert Manning as 'the luny' [sic] and had told her that she had once removed a razor from under his pillow.

After hearing conflicting evidence from the medical witnesses on their various dealings with Manning, the counsels for the prosecution and defence made their closing speeches.

Mr Acland, for the prosecution, maintained that Albert Manning had known full well what he was doing when he purchased a revolver and bullets and that, rather than insane, he was simply consumed by jealousy. He advised the jury to exercise caution in their appraisal of the evidence from Manning's relatives, reasoning that, since this was a capital crime, Manning's nearest and dearest were likely to make every possible effort to spare him from the death penalty.

For the defence, Mr Gwynne James countered by saying that the only people who were qualified to comment on Manning's mental history were his relatives and that there was no evidence that their testimony was coloured in any way by a desire to protect the prisoner. Gwynne James told the jury that he was sure that they would reach the conclusion that Manning had murdered Jane Flew but urged them to add a rider of mercy on the grounds of insanity.

It only remained for the judge to sum up the evidence. Mr Justice Grantham told the jury that however peculiar or jealous a man might appear to be, that was no justification for taking a human life. Grantham said that he personally doubted that there was anything peculiar about any of Manning's relations but that it was for the jury to determine whether or not they believed that Manning knew that what he was doing was wrong when he murdered Jane Flew. Grantham concluded his speech by adding that, as far as he was concerned, the only possible conclusion that the jury could come to was that the prisoner knew what he was doing.

It took the jury just ten minutes to agree. Manning faced the pronunciation of his death sentence with his customary disengaged silence and was removed to Gloucester Prison to await his execution.

Albert Manning was generally well liked and there was a great deal of public sympathy for his situation. A petition was raised against his execution and signed by many. However, the efforts of the petitioners came to nothing and, on 16 March 1893, Manning faced executioner William Billington and his assistant Mr Scott.

Manning maintained his elective muteness until the day before his execution, when he was visited by his mother. It was as if her visit had opened a floodgate, as he suddenly began talking again, not only to his mother but to prison governor Major Knox. On the night before his death, he conversed rationally with Knox for more than half an hour, ending the exchange by dictating three letters, one of which was to the Zion Chapel at Kingswood. Although Manning made no formal confession to the murder, he insisted to all that he died repentant and that he had found peace and comfort in his religion and was confident that his earthly sins had been forgiven by God.

Albert Manning walked briskly to the scaffold, his head erect and his lips moving in silent prayer. Those who witnessed his execution were astounded by the transformation in his demeanour. His customary dazed, vacant expression was replaced by one of intelligence and, according to the contemporary newspapers, '... all doubts as to his absolute sanity were at once removed.'

Note: In some contemporary accounts of the murder, the victim's name is given as Elizabeth Jane Flew and PC Askell is alternatively named PC Arkell. George Peach is alternatively referred to both as Jane Flew's brother and brother-in-law.

17

'WE WERE TALKING FRIENDLY AND THEN I STABBED HIM'

Wick, 1898

The driverless horse trotted skittishly past several people before it was finally brought to a halt by William Knapp, near the Carpenter's Arms pub at Wick, on the outskirts of Bristol. Knapp instantly recognised the animal as belonging to farmer James Ricketts and was understandably perturbed to find that the cart that the horse was pulling was empty.

Having secured the horse at the pub, Knapp began to walk in the direction it had come from, hoping to meet Ricketts in hot pursuit of his runaway cart. He had barely walked 150 yards when he found him lying beneath the hedge on the side of the road, bleeding heavily from wounds in his chest.

Knapp ran to fetch the Wick policeman, Acting Sergeant Charles Sims, who in turn summoned Dr H.H. Williams. The doctor arrived on the scene within minutes of Knapp's discovery but could do little more for Ricketts than to pronounce life extinct. It was evident that he had been murdered and Sims immediately began a hunt for his killer.

Sims learned that Ricketts had left his farm at about eight o'clock that morning with eight sacks of potatoes loaded on his cart, which he was intending to sell in Bristol. His son, John, had offered to accompany him but his father had declined, telling him that there was too much work to do on the farm. The sale of the potatoes should have realised the sum of £3 12s and Ricketts was known to have been carrying at least another shilling, given to him by his wife, Mary Ann, before he left home. When the police searched Ricketts' body, they found a canvas bag in his pocket containing £3 13s in silver and a further shilling in copper coins and his watch and chain were still in place. Whatever the motive for his murder, it did not seem to have been robbery.

John believed that his father would have driven to Lawrence Hill, where he would have sold his potatoes. He thought it likely that his father would then have lunched at the Earl Russell Hotel and said that he had also mentioned his intention of calling at his regular watering hole, the Lord Rodney. The police went to the Lord Rodney, where landlady Elizabeth Poole confirmed that Ricketts had indeed been drinking there on the afternoon of his death.

He had been in the company of a youth who she didn't recognise as someone who had ever visited the pub before. While Mrs Poole hadn't seen Ricketts talking to the young man, customer James Hook stated that Ricketts had treated the young man to beer, paying with money from the canvas bag, which he took from his pocket. Eventually they had left the pub together and driven off in Ricketts' cart. Unfortunately, nobody had paid much attention to the youth and could only describe him as having been in his late teens and wearing a dark grey or black coat. Several people, including policeman Isaac Howell Rees, had seen the two men in Ricketts' cart at about six o'clock that evening, but it was dark and the youth had been sitting with his back to the witnesses, so no one could add any more detail to his description.

As Ricketts and the young stranger were driving down Warmley Hill, the cart passed two pedestrians. The first, an old man named John Cryer, quite clearly heard a man's voice saying, 'Oh, you *******,' shortly after the cart passed and, moments later, someone ran by him at speed, heading in the direction of Bristol.

Just minutes earlier, Cryer had been overtaken by another pedestrian, Albert Dicks. Dicks, who was walking into Bristol for a shave and to do some shopping, had also seen the cart and noticed the driver and his passenger sitting quite close together, talking to each other. Not long after the cart passed him, Dicks heard someone saying, 'Oh, oh, oh.' It sounded to Dicks like a man groaning in pain and he stopped to listen. Within half a minute or so, a young man ran out of the darkness, coming from the direction of the cart.

'What was that noise?' the young man asked Dicks, who admitted that he didn't know.

Dicks had heard no screams or shouts for help or any sounds, other than the soft groans, to indicate that there was anything seriously amiss. He had arranged to meet someone from the tram at Kingswood and was thus in rather a hurry to continue his journey. 'I cannot go back, because I want to get to Kingswood,' Dicks told the young man, who immediately said that he too was going to Bristol and suggested that they walk together.

They had gone only a few yards when Dicks met an acquaintance walking in the opposite direction and asked him what the noise was. The man said that he had also heard something strange but didn't know what it was that he had heard.

Dicks and the young man continued to walk towards Bristol, chatting as they went. Dicks asked his companion where he had come from and was told that he had come from Pucklechurch and was heading into Bristol to see his mother. Dicks formed the impression that the stranger was an intelligent and well-educated young man but felt that he was a bit absentminded. At times, he hesitated before answering Dicks's questions and, on occasions, he didn't bother to answer at all. The man seemed in an awful hurry to get to Bristol, walking at a brisk pace and, at one stage, suggesting to Dicks that they should run for a bit.

'What say if we do a trot?' he asked Dicks, who declined, pointing out that he was wearing a heavy greatcoat and couldn't run.

Later in their journey, they met another acquaintance of Dicks, who was walking out with a young lady. The acquaintance wished Dicks 'Good night, Albert,' at which the young man looked startled.

'I thought they were speaking to me,' he explained to Dicks. 'That is my name.'

The two men reached the tram terminus at Kingswood, where Albert Dicks was expecting to meet his friend. Dicks left the young man in the waiting room and thought no more about him until he read of the murder of James Ricketts in the local newspaper. Asked by the police for a description of his companion, Dicks could only say that he was a 'mere boy'. He recalled that the youth had a fair complexion and a wispy moustache and that he was wearing a dark coat. Dicks thought that he would recognise him if he saw him again.

The police now had a suspect for the murder of James Ricketts and the hunt for the young man seen drinking with him in the pub and later riding in his cart began in earnest. Ricketts was a highly respected farmer who was not known to have any enemies, but when the police spoke to his wife she told them that, on two or three occasions since Christmas, a young man had been hanging around the farmhouse at night and had once hammered on the door. Mary Ann Ricketts said that her husband had leaned out of the bedroom window to ask what the man wanted but the caller had sneaked away without answering. Although the descriptions of the youth seen with her husband were sketchy, Mary Ann had a clear view of their mysterious caller in the moonlight and believed that he and the youth were of similar appearance. As a result of their conversation with Mary Ann Ricketts, the police interviewed several vagrants from the area but were able to eliminate all of them from their enquiries.

Meanwhile, a post-mortem examination had been conducted on James Ricketts by surgeon Henry Williams, who established that the farmer had been the victim of a frenzied attack. Ricketts had several abrasions on his face, which Williams believed had resulted from his fall from the cart. He had three knife wounds in the left-hand side of his chest, one of which had penetrated his heart, causing his almost immediate death. There was a fourth stab wound in Ricketts' abdomen and a fifth in his back, which had penetrated only as far as his spine. Although he believed that great force had been used to inflict all of the wounds, Williams described the fifth wound as the most violent of all and was of the opinion that it had been made using a different knife, with a wider blade. A butcher's knife had been found in the bottom of Ricketts' cart and Williams was certain that this could have caused all of Ricketts' wounds, with the probable exception of the one in his back. Williams also examined the clothes that Ricketts was wearing at the time of his death and discovered a further six slashes in the back of his coat where, according to the surgeon, the knife blows had gone in a downwards direction rather than inwards into Ricketts' body.

The murder was committed on 17 January 1898 and, in spite of their diligent investigations, the police were unable to trace the mysterious youth who seemed to have vanished into thin air after he was last seen by Albert Dicks at Kingswood tram terminus. However, on the evening of 25 January, the search came to a sudden and unexpected end. Nearly ninety miles from Bristol, a young man walked into a police station in Birmingham and told the surprised officers there that he wished to surrender himself for the murder of a man.

The man, who gave his name as Albert Griffiths, said that he had read about the murder in the Birmingham newspapers and knew that he had to unburden himself. He told the police that, having killed the man, he had pawned his coat in Bristol to get enough money for his fare to Birmingham. Since his arrival in the city, he had been looking for work but had so far been unable to find any.

The Birmingham Police sent a telegraph to the Gloucestershire Police that read: 'Albert Griffiths, aged 18, of 13 Church Street, Barton Hill, Bristol, has surrendered himself here for committing the murder of James Ricketts, at Wick, on Monday 17th instant. Please send for him.'

Superintendent John Matthews went to Birmingham to collect Griffiths, bringing him back to Bristol by train in an especially reserved carriage. Charged with the wilful murder of James Ricketts, Griffiths dictated a statement in which he confirmed his name, age and address, saying that he lived with his mother and his father, who was a butcher. Griffiths went on to state that he worked for fancy toy merchants Messrs Hall and Fitzgerald, in Victoria Street.

He told the police that, on 17 January, he had stolen a boning knife from his father's shop. He had gone to the Lord Rodney and enjoyed a drink with James Ricketts, accepting his offer of a lift. 'We were talking friendly and then I stabbed him,' Griffiths confessed, adding that he had not known Ricketts and, prior to meeting him in the pub, had never seen him before in his life.

He went on to say that he had not realised that he had killed the farmer until he read about the murder in the *Daily Press* the next morning. Afraid to stay in Bristol, he pawned his greatcoat and fled to Birmingham.

While at Birmingham, Griffiths was searched and a prayer book taken from his pocket. When Superintendent Matthews examined it, he found that several pages had been torn out and that others bore cryptic messages, written in the prisoner's handwriting. One read 'Killed a million of men in one room' [*sic*] and another 'Murdered 5000 pigs all by myself'.

As a result of his prisoner's statement, Matthews asked Sergeant Charles Harris to enquire at all the local pawn shops and, at Frank Witt's premises in Cumberland Street, Harris retrieved Griffiths's dark grey greatcoat. When the pockets were checked, they were found to contain an American spring knife, as well as a false moustache and nose and some stage make up, used to darken the skin. The knife was sent to public analyst George Embrey who, on testing it, found it to be bloodstained. Although Embrey couldn't determine whether the blood originated from a person or an animal, on examining the stains microscopically, he found the corpuscles to be identical to those of human blood.

An inquest was opened into Ricketts' death at the Carpenter's Arms by coroner Mr E.M. Grace. Originally opened on 19 January, it was adjourned pending the results of police enquiries, re-opening on 2 February. One of the people to testify at the inquest was John Fox, a butcher employed by Griffiths's father.

Fox told the coroner that, in the course of his work, he used a knife very similar to the one found in Ricketts' cart after his death. He had last used the knife on 15 January and, when he came to use it again on 18 January, had been unable to find it.

Questioned by the coroner, Fox told him that he had worked for Mr Griffiths for almost nineteen years and, during that time, scores of knives had gone missing and in fact more than twelve had probably been stolen in the past six months. Fox and Mr Grace became embroiled in a somewhat heated argument about the amount of wear on the knife and the fact that it would have changed shape, having been used. Eventually, Fox illustrated his answers by drawing a diagram for the coroner. There were naturally a multitude of knives at the butcher's premises and consequently he was unable to state with complete certainty that the murder weapon was the actual knife he had lost.

Fox was also asked about his impressions of Albert Griffiths and stated that he had noticed a definite change in the boy over the last three months. He had known Albert since he was born and had always found him a likeable and well-behaved lad. Yet recently, he had become rather strange and peculiar in his manner. He would sometimes talk nonsense and often had difficulty in answering questions. Fox told the inquest that, two and a half years earlier, Griffiths had suffered a serious accident and, for a time, had not been expected to survive. In addition, he had recently been hit on the head by a cricket ball.

The coroner's jury returned a verdict of wilful murder against Albert Griffiths, who was actually just seventeen years and four months old, not eighteen as had been previously believed. Meanwhile, the local paper, the *Bristol Mercury and Daily Post*, received a letter from Griffith's sister, who wanted it to be known that the false moustache and nose and stage make up found in the pocket of her brother's coat were innocent items that the family had used in party games over Christmas.

Although he had already been committed for trial on a coroner's warrant, Griffiths made his last appearance before magistrates on 4 February, where evidence was heard that cast some doubts on his sanity. His employer, Henry Edgar Fitzgerald, testified that Griffiths had been working for his company for the past four years and had been promoted to stock clerk in the leather department. Fitzgerald described Griffiths as quiet, civil, respectful and well-conducted, but stated that during the previous September, they had noticed a sudden change in his demeanour. Griffiths became totally indifferent to everything and, as a result, was given his notice, leaving the firm in November 1897. Under questioning from prosecuting counsel, Mr Wansbrough, Fitzgerald conceded that he had not noticed any signs of insanity or eccentricity in his employee but said that the youth had become callous and careless and had ceased to take notice of anything that was said to him.

Thomas Griffiths had not been aware that his son had been dismissed from his job, since the boy had continued to leave home and return every day as he always had when he was working and had also handed his wages to his mother at the end of every week. Griffiths had not found out until two days before the murder that his son had no job and was selling pigeons to make a living. However, he and his wife had accepted Albert's explanation that he had found a new position, where he would be earning an extra three shillings a week.

Griffiths said that, until three months before the murder, Albert had always been well behaved. 'There was never a better boy,' he sobbed. However, he too had noticed a distinct change in Albert's demeanour in the three months prior to the murder, stating that the boy had become dull and uncommunicative, complaining of pains in his head and back and spending much of his time lying on the sofa. Griffiths went on to confirm that there was a family history of insanity. His own uncle was twice admitted as an in-patient to the Stafford County Asylum and Albert's aunt had died in the same institution. Griffiths also spoke of two serious accidents that had befallen his son. He had received a serious blow on the head from a cricket ball and, just two and a half years ago, had fallen between a moving train and a station platform, rupturing his kidney.

Character witnesses were called in support of Albert Griffiths, including his former schoolmaster, who stated that Albert had been an outstanding pupil, probably the best the school had ever had. Without exception, everyone who spoke on his behalf considered him a respectable, well-behaved young man although those who had recently been in his company had noticed that his personality had lately changed for the worse.

The last witness to be called before the magistrates was Dr Lionel Weatherly, who had examined Griffiths at Horfield Jail. While Weatherly stopped short of declaring Griffiths to be insane, he gave his opinion that the boy was suffering from the early stages of melancholia, which would have manifested itself in morbid, uncontrollable incidents such as striking people, setting fires, breaking windows and engaging in inappropriate indecent behaviour. Weatherly believed that the murder of James Ricketts was just such an incident.

With the foundations for an insanity defence already in place, the magistrates committed Griffiths for trial at the next Gloucester Assizes. The proceedings opened on 15 February 1989, before Mr Justice Day, with Mr Gwynne James and Mr Mordaunt Snagge prosecuting and Mr J. Cranstoun defending. Albert Ricketts looked much younger than his seventeen years as he entered the dock and, as he had done throughout his earlier hearings, he almost immediately buried his face in his handkerchief and began to sob.

The prosecution did little more than relate the facts of the case, calling those witnesses who had already testified before the magistrates to repeat their recollections. As expected, defence counsel Mr Cranstoun relied heavily on an insanity defence, calling first Thomas Griffiths and then his wife, Amelia, to describe the recent changes they had noticed in their son's character.

Amelia Griffiths told the court that her son had always been a loving and affectionate boy but, for the past three months, he had cried like a baby almost every time she spoke to him. He had constantly complained of headaches and had not been able to sleep.

Mr Justice Day, 1904. (Author's collection)

James Olds, who had known Albert Griffiths for many years, said that after the accident in which he ruptured his kidney, Albert spent six weeks in hospital. 'One boy went into hospital and another came out,' stated Olds, saying that before his accident, Albert had been 'a bright, joyous youth' but that he was now sullen and morose and it was difficult to get him to speak at all.

The defence counsel called Wilfred M. Barclay, the surgeon under whose care Albert had been after his accident. Prosecution counsel, Mr Gwynne James, asked him in cross-examination whether a ruptured kidney could affect a man's personality. When Barclay said that he had never heard of such a thing, Mr Gwynne James asked if a ruptured kidney was a recognised cause of insanity.

'Not that I know of,' Barclay replied.

Dr Lionel Weatherly was next to take the stand and was asked by the defence counsel if he had formed any opinion about the defendant's state of mind at the time of the murder.

Mr Justice Day immediately interrupted before the doctor could respond, telling Mr Cranstoun that he must rephrase his question. It was for the jury to decide the defendant's state of mind at the time of the offence and Weatherly could only give his opinion on the state of his mind when he interviewed him in Horfield Jail.

Mr Cranstoun made several attempts at rephrasing his question, none of which satisfied Mr Justice Day, who repeatedly refused to allow the doctor to answer. Eventually, Day told Cranstoun rather impatiently, 'Get out the fact that he was insane at Horfield and then you can argue that the insanity probably did not come out in one night.'

'He may have been perfectly sane at Horfield and insane before,' argued Cranstoun.

'Then you must take the consequences and call witnesses to show that he was insane then,' thundered the judge.

'I cannot do that,' replied Cranstoun.

'You can ask the witness what opinion he formed as to the state of the prisoner's mind at Horfield,' said Day, helpfully.

'I cannot go upon that entirely,' interjected Dr Weatherly. 'No medical man can give an opinion as to insanity merely upon what he is told by the person himself.'

'Do you say you found him insane at Horfield?' asked the judge.

'I could not say that,' replied the doctor.

Cranstoun was allowed to ask the doctor some questions about his interview with Albert Griffiths at Horfield Jail but could only get an admission from Weatherly that Griffiths was depressed and in the early stages of melancholia. In other words, he was not insane.

The prosecution then called Dr F.H. Craddock, the medical superintendent of the Gloucester County Lunatic Asylum, who, having had several interviews with Griffiths, stated that the defendant had never shown the least signs of insanity. The police officers who had dealt with Griffiths at both Birmingham and Bristol had already stated that, although he was depressed and tearful, he had shown no signs of insanity whatsoever.

In his closing speech, Mr Cranstoun asked that the jury think carefully about the question of insanity. Griffiths had never met the victim until shortly before the murder, so could have borne him no malice and although Griffiths had only a shilling to his name and was aware that Ricketts was carrying a large sum of money about his person, not a penny piece was stolen. A man was assumed sane in the eyes of the law unless it could be proved otherwise but, Cranstoun asked, how could he prove it? Surely the fact that the murder of James Ricketts was so completely without motive meant that the defendant would have had to have been insane to kill him? Cranstoun reminded the jury that Griffiths had gone away for more than a week after the murder and that nobody had been given the chance to examine him during that crucial time. He addressed the family history and asked if the recent changes in his behaviour might be the beginnings of hereditary insanity, stressing that the only reason for Ricketts' murder was that Griffiths had suffered an uncontrollable impulse and had been unable to restrain himself.

Mr Gwynne James gave a closing speech for the prosecution, arguing that Griffiths's actions after the murder were those of a sane man. He had pawned his coat to obtain money and fled the area – why would he have done that if he had not realised the nature and quality of his acts? Gwynne James gestured to the prisoner in the dock, telling the jury that he seemed perfectly sane now – if the murder was an irresistible impulse that heralded the onset of insanity, shouldn't he have become even more insane in the time since the murder? As for not stealing any money from the victim, the defendant had, in all probability, realised that there were people nearby and made a decision to run away before he had time to steal anything.

In his summing up of the evidence for the jury, Mr Justice Day stated that none of the witnesses who had been called had been able to demonstrate a single sign of insanity in the accused. Day advised the jury to ignore the strange writings in Griffiths's prayer book, saying that there was no evidence that they were genuine and they might well have been written for the express purpose of relying on an insanity defence.

The jury took just eight minutes to find Albert Griffiths 'Guilty' of the wilful murder of James Ricketts, although they recommended mercy on the grounds of his youth. Griffiths sobbed bitterly as the judge pronounced the death sentence, his extreme distress affecting everybody in court.

His execution date was set for 9 March but immediately after the trial a petition was raised in protest against the sentence. On 22 February, the *Bristol Mercury and Daily Post* published a lengthy editorial in which the writer agreed that the case was worthy of further consideration by Home Secretary Sir Matthew White Ridley but on the grounds of questions about the prisoner's sanity rather than his youth.

This was not a crime for which the hot blood of youth could be held responsible, stated the newspaper:

> If it had been committed through love or jealousy or in the excitement of an inexperi-
> enced mind intoxicated with worldly pleasures, youth would have been some excuse

Parkhurst Prison, Isle of Wight. (Author's collection)

but the slaughter of an inoffensive old man, who was actually performing a neigh-bourly act to his murderer, is so wanton that, if it is the act of an unquestionably sane person, he deserves to suffer for it like a man-eating tiger.

In the event, the Home Secretary commuted the death sentence to one of life imprisonment although, interestingly, Griffiths seems to have served at least part of his sentence in Parkhurst Prison on the Isle of Wight rather than at a criminal lunatic asylum such as Broadmoor.

Note: In the contemporary newspaper accounts of the murder, the man who caught Ricketts' horse and later found his body is named as both William Knapp and Francis Tippings. The name Tippings appears only in the earliest reports, while later accounts refer to William Knapp 'and others' finding the body. To avoid confusion, I have used only the name Knapp. Witness John Cryer is also named as Charles Cryer.

18

'LET'S HAVE ANOTHER DRINK'

Temple, 1899

Fredrick William Hayball and his wife, Ellen Scudder Hayball, were no strangers to the police courts in Bristol. They married in 1886 and soon began a cycle of separation and reconciliation, the periods during which they lived as man and wife punctuated with continuous drunkenness and domestic violence. In February 1894, Ellen was charged with feloniously wounding her husband when, after a day spent drinking, she attacked Fred on the street and knocked him down. Ellen's brother was quick to pile into the fray and before long the two men were engaged in a violent fight.

When they were eventually pulled apart, Fred set off to walk home, with Ellen following on behind him. With hindsight, Fred might have been wiser to keep his wife in view since Ellen suddenly ran at him and stabbed him twice in the back. As he tried to ward off a third blow from the knife, Fred's hand was badly cut. Weakened by loss of blood, he managed to make his way home, where Ellen promptly hit him over the head with a teacup and then threw a chair at him.

Fred staggered to the nearest police station, from where he was escorted to the Bristol General Hospital. Although his wounds were not serious, he was admitted as a precaution and remained a patient for four days.

On his discharge from hospital, Fred made a formal complaint against his wife, who consequently appeared before magistrates at Bristol Police Court in March 1894. The case unfolded to reveal a tragic tale of a desperately unhappy marriage, with Fred swearing that Ellen had stabbed him twice before and had also stabbed his dog. Ellen was represented by solicitor Mr Hugh Holmes Gore, who countered Fred's allegations by informing the magistrates that he had twice been imprisoned for assaulting his wife and that Ellen had now obtained a separation order against him. Eventually the magistrates decided that, although they could not dispute the fact that Fred had been wounded, there was insufficient evidence to prove that it had been Ellen who was responsible and she was discharged.

In December 1896, it was Fred's turn to appear at Bristol Police Court on a charge of ill-treating the couple's two young sons. On 15 December, he drunkenly thrashed nine-year-old Frederick George and his eight-year-old brother Samuel. Fred junior's eye was injured and Samuel's legs were so badly bruised that, ten days later, he was still able to show the magistrates the terrible consequences of the vicious beating he had received from his father. Once again, solicitor Mr Gore was involved, this time prosecuting the case for the Society for the Prevention of Cruelty to Children.

Fred maintained that he had only beaten the boys to chastise them, after discovering that Fred junior had been 'mooching off' school for two weeks. The magistrates remarked that the children no doubt needed chastisement but not in the extreme manner chosen by their father, who was sentenced to seven days hard labour for his harsh disciplinary methods.

Fred later served a three-month prison sentence for beating Ellen and, on the very night that he was released from prison, he beat her again. Early in 1899, Ellen took out a summons against Fred for kicking her in the head. However, Fred failed to appear in court to answer the charge against him, telling Ellen that if she ever dared to speak out again, he would take a knife to her and kill her.

By May 1899, Fred and Ellen were living in lodgings in Jones's Court, off Avon Street, in Temple. The area was, according to the *Bristol Mercury and Daily Post*, 'at the heart of a thickly populated working class district' and was 'not a pleasant place' and the Hayballs' house, with its rag-stuffed broken windows and dark, squalid rooms, was especially wretched. By now, the couple had five children together but only the youngest – a two-year-old girl – was living with them. One child had been adopted and two more – presumably Fred junior and Samuel – were living at the Bristol Guardian's Boys' Home on Cumberland Road. (The whereabouts of the fifth child are not recorded.) The Hayballs' home was notorious in the neighbourhood as being the scene of constant loud, drink-fuelled arguments.

On the night of 20 May, two patrolling police officers met Ellen walking in Avon Street, her little girl on her hip. After wishing the policemen 'Good evening,' Ellen remarked to them that she and her husband lived in the area. 'Look what the pretty beauty has done,' she instructed the constables, showing them her hand, which was badly bruised. 'He accused me of going with other men,' she explained, before the police had to leave her in order to deal with a fight that had broken out further along the road. Ellen had spoken to her next-door neighbour, Mrs Gilks, earlier that evening, telling her that Fred had not yet come home from his work as a dock labourer with his wages and that she was going to find him before he drank all their money. At the same time, Ellen also told Laura Gilks that she was feeling very depressed and that she thought she might be pregnant and she particularly asked her neighbour to call her the following day at midday, if she overslept.

Mrs Gilks saw Fred and Ellen returning home a little later and unusually, there were no raised voices and no quarrel between them that night. What was unusual was that the following morning, Fred was seen going back and forth to the communal tap for buckets of water, a task he normally left for his wife to do.

Temple Church. (Author's collection)

Fred's suspicious activities had not gone unnoticed by the other residents of the small court and, as there was no sign of Ellen, Mrs Floyd went to Laura Gilks and suggested that someone should check on her. Mindful that Ellen had specifically asked to be called if she should happen to oversleep, Laura kept a watchful eye on the Hayballs' house until she saw Fred leave. Then, asking Mrs Floyd to keep watch in case he returned, she went next door and called for Ellen several times. There was no answer and Laura was instantly concerned. From what Ellen had told her only the day before, Laura believed that she was desperately unhappy about the possibility that she might be pregnant and feared that she might be lying ill indoors, having tried to abort her unborn child.

Laura went into the house to see if Ellen was all right. There was no sign of her in the kitchen or living room downstairs, so Laura went upstairs. The bedroom door was closed and a folded pamphlet had been used to wedge it shut. Laura managed to push it open a few inches but, as soon as she did, a foul smell assaulted her nostrils and she suddenly felt very afraid. Without looking into the bedroom, she ran downstairs and out of the house, where Mrs Floyd and another neighbour, Emily Jenkins, were anxiously waiting for her.

'You are a braver woman,' Laura said to Emily Jenkins. 'You go first.'

Cautiously Emily crept up the stairs and pushed the bedroom door fully open, Laura Gilks at her heels.

'She's not on the bed,' Emily said, before she spotted Ellen Hayball lying apparently dead on the floor of her bedroom, a piece of sacking over her face.

The two women fled out of the house yelling 'Police!' and 'Murder!' When they reached the court outside, it occurred to them that Ellen might possibly still be alive and they bravely went back into the house to see if they could help her. Sadly, it was too late. Dressed only in her chemise, Ellen Hayball was stiff and cold and, when Emily peeled back the piece of sacking, it revealed a face covered in dried blood. Ellen had two deep cuts over her right eye exposing her brain and a badly cut ear, with two more wounds immediately behind it. When surgeon Henry T. Rudge later conducted a post-mortem examination on Ellen's body, he also found that she was black and blue, with bruises almost all over her body.

Meanwhile, PC Albert White was patrolling his beat on Victoria Street when he heard some children excitedly saying that there was somebody dead in a court off Avon Street. White went to investigate, meeting Laura Gilks as she rushed to summon the police to the Hayballs' house.

White was soon joined at Jones's Court by PC Shearn and Sergeant Little. As White began a search of the house, he asked Laura if she knew where Ellen's husband was.

'I could dap my hand on him in a minute,' replied Laura, who had earlier seen Fred heading towards the nearby Cross Guns Tavern.

Laura hurried towards the pub in search of Fred Hayball, thinking that the policeman was following her. Sure enough, Fred was there drinking beer. He seemed unconcerned when Laura told him that his wife was dying and asked him to come home at once. 'Let's have another drink,' he said calmly, adding, 'I'll be home in five minutes.'

Without waiting for Fred, Laura went back to Jones's Court to tell the police that she had found him. PC White and Sergeant Little immediately went to the Cross Guns but, by the time they got there, Fred had gone. Landlord George White told them that, having spoken to Laura, Fred had left almost at once.

A search of the house at Jones's Court by Inspector Johnson and Detective Inspector Robertson revealed a small hatchet in a stone sink in the kitchen. The hatchet, which was covered with a piece of wet sacking, had obviously been recently washed and, when it was later sent to public analyst Frederick Wallis Stoddart, he theorised that it had been cleaned using hot water and bread. Stoddart was able to find traces of blood on the hatchet, although he could not determine whether the stains originated from an animal or a human being. Shown the hatchet, surgeon Henry Rudge determined that it was most probably the murder weapon.

An inquest was opened into Ellen Hayball's death at the police station in Bedminster, under the direction of deputy coroner Mr A.E. Barker. Everyone who had been involved in the aftermath of the murder gave evidence, as did Ellen Hayball's sister, Mrs Minnie Martha Pocock, who confirmed that Ellen had led a wretched life and that the news of her murder had come as no surprise, since she had been expecting it now for some years.

Mrs Pocock related some of the worst incidences of violence between the couple throughout their marriage, telling the inquest that her sister was terrified of Fred. When asked why Ellen persisted in taking her husband back in the face of such dreadful abuse, Minnie stated that Ellen had a particularly forgiving nature and was concerned about the fate of her children. Minnie also revealed that she now had custody of her two-year-old niece, who was found playing alone on the front doorstep of the house, while her mother lay brutally murdered inside.

The one notable absentee from the inquest was Fred Hayball, who hadn't been seen since he left the Cross Guns Tavern after being informed by Laura Gilks of his wife's condition. Fred was an ex-sailor and the police placed a watch on the ports at Cardiff, Newport and Swansea, in case he had managed to board a ship in Bristol. Officers searched diligently for him, both on foot and on bicycles and every policeman in Bristol received a description of the missing man, who was said to be 'five feet eight or nine inches in height, stoutly built with a fresh, clean shaven complexion. When last seen, he was wearing a dark coat with a patch on one of the shoulders, moleskin trousers, a white muffler with blue spots and a cloth cap.'

There had been numerous sightings of a man of similar appearance and countless rumours about his present whereabouts. His body had been found in the Floating Harbour at Bristol. He had been seen aboard a pleasure steamer at the Cumberland Basin. He had tried to sleep by a night watchman's fire. He had been spotted on the quay and around the docks where he worked. The police thoroughly investigated every possible sighting but were unable to establish that any of them had been of Frederick Hayball. Thus, he was not present at the inquest to hear the coroner's jury return a verdict of wilful murder against him.

Rumours about Fred continued to spread through Bristol like wildfire. He was reported to have been arrested in Plymouth and a crowd of around 2,000 people gathered at Temple Meads Station to witness his return to Bristol by train. Even after waiting for more than two and a half hours, the crowd were reluctant to believe officials, who assured them that there had been no arrest. Before long, a rumour that he had been arrested in Cardiff caused similar excitement. Unfortunately, the gossip was totally without foundation and Frederick William Hayball was never knowingly seen again, either dead or alive.

In March 1904, there was a curious twist in the case when a man named John Morgan was arrested in Salford, now a borough in Greater Manchester but then an important town in its own right. Questioned on charges of attempting to obtain money by false pretences from a seaman's outfitter on the Trafford Road, Morgan suddenly seemed to feel the need to unburden himself of a far more serious crime. 'I may as well tell you the truth,' he told the interviewing officer. 'At Bristol in May 1899, I hit my wife over the head with a hatchet then went away to sea. I don't know what became of her, or whether she is living or not.' Having made his statement, the man signed it 'Frederick William Hayball.'

Bristol Temple Meads Station. (Author's collection)

Having looked back through the *Police Gazette*, Chief Detective Inspector Heath found that a Mrs Hayball had indeed been murdered in May 1899 and that her husband, Frederick William Hayball, was wanted in connection with her death. Heath contacted his colleagues at Bristol, who immediately sent an officer to Salford to interview John Morgan. However, the Bristol officer was able to report that Morgan was definitely not Frederick William Hayball and the confession was therefore dismissed as a hoax.

19

'IT MIGHT BE ONLY A CURIOUS COINCIDENCE'

Crew's Hole / St Augustine's, 1915

Around the turn of the twentieth century, the area of the river Avon known as Crew's Hole was the site of numerous chemical factories, smelting works and tar distilleries. In 1883, the *Bristol Times and Mirror* printed an article on Crew's Hole, the reporter describing it thus:

> Here there are no palatial buildings. It is all hard grimy reality. The huge mounds of refuse that put one in mind of miniature mountains, the tall brick chimneys, the great wooden structures black with creosote that rise here and there like castles, the long rows of shedding, have nothing of the poetical about them.

A bustling, noxious and highly industrialised area, it was the place where William George Jefferies met his death.

The thirty-seven-year-old labourer's body was pulled from the river at Crew's Hole in July 1915. Initially his death seemed like a tragic accident and it was first assumed that he had simply stumbled into the water and drowned. However, a post-mortem examination, conducted by Dr Lucas and Dr Foss, revealed some surprising results.

The two doctors found a series of wounds on Jefferies's head, which they believed had been made by a sharp instrument, such as a chisel. The wounds formed a definite pattern and, according to the doctors, could not possibly have been self-inflicted. Although Jefferies had indeed died from drowning, the doctors believed that the wounds had been inflicted just a few minutes before his death and, even though his skull wasn't fractured, they were sufficiently severe to have stunned him. He would therefore have entered the water in 'a dazed condition', if not unconscious, making it impossible for him to save himself from drowning.

An inquest was held, which failed to discover any logical reason for William Jefferies's demise. According to his wife, he was a very strong swimmer. He had not been drinking, did not appear to have been robbed and was not known to have any enemies, or to have engaged in any quarrels or arguments prior to his death. Nobody in the area had seen anything suspicious and, when the inquest closed on 16 August 1915, the jury were only able to record a verdict of 'Found drowned in the River Avon whilst suffering from wounds in the head, there being no evidence to show how the wounds were caused.' There the matter might have rested, if Dr Lucas had not been asked to conduct a post-mortem examination on the victim of another sudden death.

St Augustine's. (Author's collection)

St Augustine's Gateway. (Author's collection)

On 21 July 1915, the body of Sidney George Hawker was found at the bottom of some steps of a building in St Augustine's. Initially, it looked as though the seventeen-year-old porter had died as a result of a fall down the steps, since blood and hair were found on the door of the premises and on the stairs. However, when Dr Lucas examined the body, he was mystified to see an all too familiar pattern of wounds on the top and back of Hawker's skull and behind one ear.

The wounds were almost identical in shape and pattern to those found on the skull of William Jefferies. Again, there were no fractures to Hawker's skull, just the strangely shaped wounds which, according to Dr Lucas, had been inflicted from behind the victim, using a chisel or similar pointed instrument.

The police were unable to identify anyone who might have inflicted these wounds. The only evidence that emerged from their enquiries was that a postman delivering letters to the building on the morning of Sidney Hawker's death had seen two men loitering outside the premises, acting as if they didn't wish to be seen. However, in spite of extensive investigations by the police, these men were never located.

On 20 August, the coroner held an inquest on the death of Sidney Hawker. He questioned Dr Lucas extensively about the marked similarity between the two deaths and Lucas told him that, in each case, there were no fractures of the skull. Both men had a pattern of parallel wounds on their heads, which were in roughly the same position and all of the wounds seemed to have been inflicted from behind with a similar sharp instrument, such as a chisel. 'It might be only a curious coincidence,' stated the doctor.

'If it is a coincidence, it is a most remarkable one,' concluded the coroner.

The inquest jury returned a verdict of 'murder by some person or persons unknown' on the death of Sidney George Hawker. There was no evidence to suggest that he and William Jefferies had known each other in life and the two men appeared to have no acquaintances or activities in common.

Nobody was ever charged with either murder and 'The Two Bristol Mysteries', as they were referred to in the contemporary newspapers, remain unexplained.

Note: In some contemporary accounts of his murder, Sidney Hawker's forename is alternatively spelled Sydney, while Crew's Hole is also named as Crews Hole.

20

'SHE RILED ME SO THAT I LOST MY HEAD'

Failand, 1926

Thirty-five-year-old Sarah Louise Emily Rowles was the daughter of a farm labourer from Failand on the outskirts of Bristol, a short distance away from the foot of the Clifton Suspension Bridge. A bright and normally cheerful woman, Sarah served as a land girl during the First World War and, by 1926, was working with her mother as a laundress and was also the regular organist and cleaner at the Wesleyan Chapel in Failand.

Twelve years earlier, Sarah, who was unmarried, had given birth to an illegitimate son. She refused to reveal the name of the child's father and would only say that he was a man who was employed at Failand Hill. In the strict moral climate of the day, this was seen as an 'unfortunate circumstance' by her family and, having thus blotted her copybook, Sarah's father made sure that he kept a very close eye on her from then onwards. She still lived with her parents, along with her son and three other children that her parents had adopted, and was not usually allowed out at night unless she was accompanied by either her mother or father.

On Friday, 12 March 1926, Sarah's mother left the family home to take her grandson on a short holiday, leaving Sarah to handle the outstanding laundry. By the time her father returned from work, she had almost finished for the day and, as he was pottering in the garden, she called out to him, 'I am going now, Dad,' which he took to mean that she was intending to deliver her finished laundry back to its owners.

The laundry loaded into a little handcart, James Rowles watched his daughter set off, accompanied by her two adopted brothers. However, some time later, the two boys returned home alone, pulling the empty truck and, when Rowles asked them where 'Auntie Sarah' was, they told him that she had gone for a little walk and would be back soon. James assumed that Sarah had gone to visit her aunt and, when she hadn't returned home by nine o'clock that evening he went to bed, leaving a light burning in the kitchen. To his surprise, when he got up the next morning, the light was still burning and Sarah's bed hadn't been slept in.

Meanwhile, gamekeeper Edgar Bowley was walking the Tyntesfield estate when he came across the body of a woman. She lay on her back under a tree in a field named the Bowling Green, her arms outstretched and her hair matted with dried blood. The immediate area around the body showed signs that a tremendous struggle had taken place, as if the woman had fought desperately for her life, which was confirmed by a number of cuts on her hands, apparently caused when she tried to grasp a knife or similar weapon.

Dr G.A. Valentine was called to the scene, arriving at 9.15 a.m. He found that the woman had a deep wound above her left eyebrow that was almost one and a half inches long, as well as a smaller cut on the top of her nose. She was wearing a fur stole, the end of which had been thrust deep into her mouth. As far as the doctor could ascertain, she had been dead for between ten and twelve hours and there were no indications that she had been either sexually assaulted or robbed.

With Sarah Rowles known to be missing from home, her father was called to the field and quickly identified the dead woman as his daughter. The body was removed to the Flax Bourton Poor Law Institution, where Dr Valentine later assisted at a post-mortem examination carried out by Professor Walker Hall, the Professor of Pathology at Bristol University. It was determined that Sarah had died from suffocation, after part of her broken dentures lodged in her throat and choked her. The doctors were also able to confirm that she was pregnant.

Clifton Suspension Bridge, 1936. (Author's collection)

Bristol University, 1950s. (Author's collection)

As the police began to search the area for clues to the identity of Sarah's killer it became evident that she had not been attacked where she died. A broken knife blade was found at the site of the initial assault and it seemed that Sarah – a strong, well-built woman – had fought off her attacker and managed to run almost sixty yards towards the safety of her home. The police found themselves baffled by Sarah's murder. She had not been robbed or sexually assaulted and, according to her father, had no male acquaintances and no enemies whatsoever, either male or female. Hence they almost immediately requested assistance from Scotland Yard, which came in the form of Chief Inspector Collins, who arrived on 14 March. Yet, by the time Collins reached Flax Bourton station, the local police had already identified and arrested a possible suspect.

The Rowles family were on very friendly terms with the Goulds, who lived in Tyntesfield Cottages and both families frequently visited each others homes socially. On the day that Sarah's body was found, Mrs Gould was quick to call on James Rowles to offer her condolences. She told James Rowles that her son, Wilfred, had been to his house that morning to see him but that Rowles had been out. Indeed, Wilfred turned up at the Rowles' house later that night to escort his mother home. He shook hands with James Rowles and answered his polite question 'How is your father?' but there was no further conversation between the two men.

What Elizabeth Gould neglected to tell James Rowles at the time was that Sarah had recently spoken to her husband, accusing twenty-one-year-old Wilfred Gould of being the father of her unborn child. Mr Gould had confronted his son with Sarah's accusation and Wilfred, who was courting a young woman from a nearby village, vehemently denied responsibility for Sarah's pregnancy, telling his father that he had barely seen her in the past year and had certainly not been intimately involved with her.

The news of a possible relationship between the murder victim and Wilfred Henry Gould sent the police straight to his house to question him. Sergeant Dunster and PC Hiscox asked him to show them the clothes that he had been wearing on the day of the murder. Gould handed over a pair of khaki-coloured trousers and a jacket for their inspection but, by chance, PC Hiscox had seen Gould shortly before the murder was thought to have been committed and immediately recognised that the jacket produced by Gould was not the one he had been wearing at the time. A search was made of Gould's room and a sports jacket was retrieved from beneath his mattress. The jacket appeared to be spotted with blood and, in spite of his denials that he was anywhere near the scene of the murder, Wilfred Gould was taken into custody on suspicion of having killed Sarah Rowles.

For a while, Gould continued to deny any involvement in Sarah's murder but in the early hours of the morning after his arrest, he suddenly blurted out to PC Hiscox, 'Look here, Mr Hiscox, I had an excuse for doing this.' He went on to tell the constable that he had met Sarah at about eight o'clock on the evening of 12 March and that she had accused him of being the father of her unborn child and demanded to know what he was going to do about it. When Wilfred denied any responsibility

An un-named police sergeant. (Author's collection)

for the pregnancy, Sarah threatened to commit suicide and make it very clear that Wilfred had driven her to do so. 'She riled me so that I lost my head,' Wilfred continued, telling Hiscox that he had taken out his knife, opened it and struck Sarah twice on the head. 'I did not know that I had killed her. I didn't intend to kill her,' he concluded.

Having made his statement, Wilfred was formally charged with the wilful murder of Sarah Rowles, appearing before magistrates at Flax Bourton on 26 March. His solicitor insisted that, if the magistrates saw fit to send his client for trial, the charge against him should be reduced to one of manslaughter on the grounds that there was no malice aforethought. However, the magistrates stated that they did not look upon themselves as a jury and were therefore not willing to take the responsibility of reducing the charge.

Thus Wilfred Gould appeared before Mr Justice Roche at the Somerset Assizes in Wells charged with the wilful murder of Sarah Rowles. The case was prosecuted by Mr Rayner Goddard KC, with the assistance of Mr H.G. Garland, while Rowles was defended by Mr F.E. Weatherly KC and Mr F. Cyril Williams.

Mr Goddard began by describing the finding of Sarah's body and the subsequent arrest of Wilfred Gould on suspicion of her murder. He told the jury that they would probably be asked to decide whether any circumstances could be found in the case that would reduce the crime from murder to manslaughter but insisted that the prosecution could see nothing whatsoever in the evidence to merit such a reduction. Goddard told the court that the crux of the case was the allegation made by Sarah Rowles that the defendant was the father of her unborn child, something that Gould continued to deny emphatically.

The prosecution maintained that Sarah had arranged to meet Gould to discuss her pregnancy and, at that meeting, there was a verbal dispute which culminated in Gould attacking Sarah with a knife. She had fought hard against the attack, cutting her hands as she tried to wrest the knife from Gould's grasp and eventually breaking free and running towards her home. Gould followed her and punched her in the face, knocking her to the ground. In an effort to stop her screaming, he had thrust her fur stole into her mouth with such violence that part of her upper denture had broken and lodged in her throat.

James Rowles was called to give evidence, telling the court that he had not suspected for one moment that his daughter might be pregnant again. He was therefore unaware that she had communicated with Mr Gould, accusing his son of being responsible for her condition, although he recalled that she had written some letters about a week before her death. Rowles admitted that Sarah was on friendly terms with the Gould family and that she had visited their house frequently but he could only recall one occasion on which she was alone with Wilfred Gould, which had been more than a year before her death. After a visit to the Goulds, Wilfred had escorted Sarah part of the way home, even though her father had arranged to collect her, and James met Sarah returning home with Wilfred on the public footpath that crossed the Bowling Green field, roughly 100 yards from where her body would later be found. Rowles repeated his claim that, in view of Sarah's 'unfortunate circumstances' he had kept her 'under his eye' and had taken great care to ensure that she did not go out at night unless she was accompanied by himself or her mother.

Gould's defence counsel insisted that Sarah had initiated the physical violence between the couple on the night of her death. Mindful of her condition and of her strict father's likely reaction to a second 'mistake', Sarah had been determined to force somebody to take responsibility for her unborn child and Wilfred, who was fourteen years her junior, had probably seemed an easy target. Faced with his refusal to have any part in her scheme, she had physically attacked him and Wilfred had pulled out his knife to defend himself. Sarah had been wounded only because she struggled to take the knife way from him and he had been reluctant to relinquish it, afraid of what she might do once she had it in her possession.

Royal Courts of Justice (Court of Appeal), London, 1940s. (Author's collection)

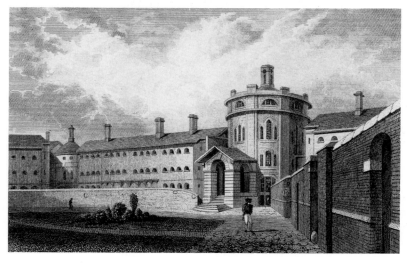

Maidstone Gaol, Kent. (Author's collection)

Rather than Sarah fleeing the scene of her attack, the defence insisted that Wilfred Gould had walked away and that Sarah had followed him and tried to physically restrain him and prevent him from leaving. In the course of Gould's struggles to escape, Sarah had been punched in the face and had fallen to the floor.

Wilfred Gould took the stand in his own defence, describing just such a scenario. He insisted that Sarah had attacked him and admitted only to defending himself against her and to trying to stop her screaming by pushing her fur stole into her mouth. According to Wilfred Gould, he had walked away from Sarah Rowles leaving her lying on the ground, still breathing and very much alive.

Having heard all the evidence, the jury were indeed asked by Mr Weatherly to reduce the charge from one of murder to manslaughter. However, after deliberating for thirty minutes, they concurred with the prosecution and returned a verdict of 'guilty of wilful murder' against Wilfred Gould. Mr Justice Roche passed the mandatory death sentence, at which the defence immediately announced their intention to appeal.

Mr Weatherly applied to the Court of Criminal Appeal for leave to challenge the conviction and the application was considered by Mr Justice Sankey, Mr Justice Talbot and Mr Justice MacKinnon in June 1926. Weatherly contended that, in his summing up of the evidence for the jury, Mr Justice Roche had not satisfactorily explained to them that the medical evidence concerning Sarah Rowles's knife wounds wholly supported Gould's account of the first encounter between them. Moreover, Gould denied knowing that Sarah Rowles had false teeth and could not therefore have anticipated that her dentures would break when he struck her face and ultimately cause her death. Furthermore, the defence insisted that the fact that Sarah Rowles had provoked the attack on her by Wilfred Gould both verbally and physically was in itself sufficient justification for a reduction of the charge against him from murder to manslaughter.

In considering Weatherly's request, Mr Justice Sankey stated that the Appeal Court Judges had reviewed Mr Justice Roche's summary and found it to be extraordinarily fair. They rejected Weatherly's suggestion that matters of self-defence and provocation had not been satisfactorily addressed, saying that the law had quite clearly and correctly been put before the jury and that they were therefore refusing the application to appeal Gould's conviction. However, less than two weeks later, it was announced that Wilfred Henry Gould had been reprieved.

In May 1931, the *Guardian* printed an article about a Lancashire man, sixty-six-year-old William Robinson. Having read about the murder in the newspapers, Robinson became intrigued by the case and requested permission to visit Wilfred Gould at Maidstone Prison, where he was serving his life sentence. The two men formed an unlikely friendship and, according to the *Guardian*, Robinson wrote to Wilfred Gould every month and always spent his annual holiday from work visiting him in prison and afterwards visiting his family in Somerset.

BIBLIOGRAPHY

Newspapers

Bristol Mercury and Daily Post
Bristol Times and Mirror
Daily Press
Guardian
Pall Mall Gazette
The Times
Western Daily Press

Various websites have also been consulted during the compilation of this book. However, since they have a tendency to disappear without notice, to avoid disappointment, they have not been individually listed.

INDEX

Other titles published by The History Press

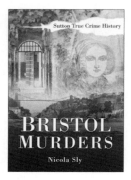

Bristol Murders
NICOLA SLY

Contained within the pages of *Bristol Murders* are the stories behind some of the most heinous crimes ever committed in Bristol. They include the murder and suicide of a brother and sister in 1842; the tragic death of 10-year-old Mabel Price in 1897; and the suspicious death of sexual deviant Cecil Cornock, which led to his wife Ann being charged with his murder and sebsequent acquittal in 1946. Nicola Sly's carefully researched, well-illustrated and enthralling text will appeal to anyone interested in the shady side of Bristol's history, and should give much food for thought.

978 0 7509 5048 0

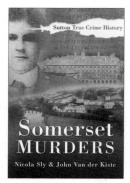

Somerset Murders
NICOLA SLY & JOHN VAN DER KISTE

Somerset Murders brings together numerous murderous tales that shocked not only the county but also made headlines throughout the country. They include the cases of Elizabeth and Betty Branch, a mother and daughter who beat a young servant girl to death in Hemington in 1740; 13-year-old Betty Trump, whose throat was cut while walking home at Buckland St Mary in 1823; and George Watkins, killed in a bare knuckle fight outside the Running Horse pub in Yeovil in 1843. This carefully researched, well-illustrated and enthralling text will appeal to anyone interested in the shady side of Somerset's history.

978 0 7509 4795 4

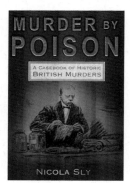

Murder by Poison: A Casebook of Historic British Murders
NICOLA SLY

Readily obtainable and almost undetectable prior to advances in forensic science during the twentieth century, poison was considered the ideal method of murder and many of its exponents failed to stop at just one victim. Along with the most notorious cases of murder by poison in the country – such as those of Mary Ann Cotton and Dr Thomas Neil Cream – this book also features many of the cases that did not make national headlines, examining not only the methods and motives but also the real stories of the perpetrators and their victims.

978 0 7524 5065 0

Haunted Bristol
SUE LE'QUEUX

From paranormal manifestations at the Bristol Old Vic to the ghostly activity of a grey monk who is said to haunt Bristol's twelfth-century cathedral, this spine-tingling collection of supernatural tales is sure to appeal to anyone interested in Bristol's haunted heritage. This enthralling selection of newspaper reports and first-hand accounts recalls strange and spooky happenings in the city's ancient streets, churches, theatres and public houses.

978 0 7524 3300 4

Visit our website and discover thousands of other History Press books.
www.thehistorypress.co.uk